MAVERICK
IN MAUVE

Adele and Jay on their honeymoon at Biltmore, in North Carolina, with her uncle George Vanderbilt (left).

MAVERICK IN MAUVE

The Diary of a Romantic Age

Florence Adele Sloane

WITH A COMMENTARY BY

Louis Auchincloss

DOUBLEDAY & COMPANY, INC.

GARDEN CITY, NEW YORK

1983

Library of Congress Cataloging in Publication Data
Sloane, Florence Adele, 1873–1960
    Maverick in mauve.

    1. Sloane, Florence Adele, 1873–1960.   2. United
States–Biography.   3. Upper classes–New York (N.Y.)
–Biography.   4. New York (N.Y.)–Biography.
I. Auchincloss, Louis.   II. Title.
CT275.S523523A35   1983   974.7′104′0924 [B]
ISBN: 0-385-19000-X
Library of Congress Catalog Card Number 82–45835

Foreword

Florence Adele Sloane, a lifetime resident of New York City, was born in 1873 and died in 1960. She was married first to James A. Burden, Jr., in 1895, and second to Richard M. Tobin, in 1936.

Louis Auchincloss married her granddaughter Adele Lawrence.

The illustrations, with a few exceptions, are all taken from family albums.

Contents

Sloane Genealogy

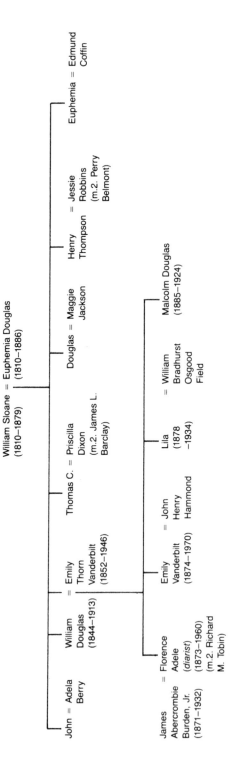

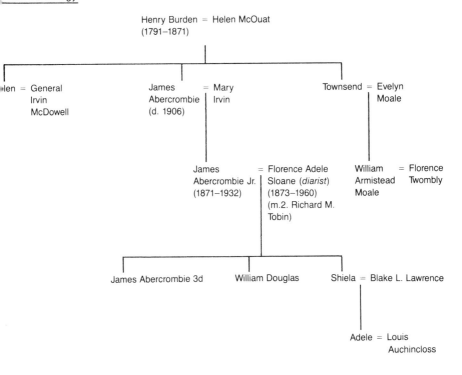

Henry Burden = Helen McOuat
(1791–1871)

...len = General
Irvin
McDowell

James = Mary
Abercrombie Irvin
(d. 1906)

Townsend = Evelyn
Moale

James = Florence Adele
Abercrombie Jr. Sloane (*diarist*)
(1871–1932) (1873–1960)
(m.2. Richard M.
Tobin)

William = Florence
Armistead Twombly
Moale

James Abercrombie 3d   William Douglas   Shiela = Blake L. Lawrence

Adele = Louis
Auchincloss

Vanderbilt Genealogy (only those descendants mentioned in text or illustrations appear)

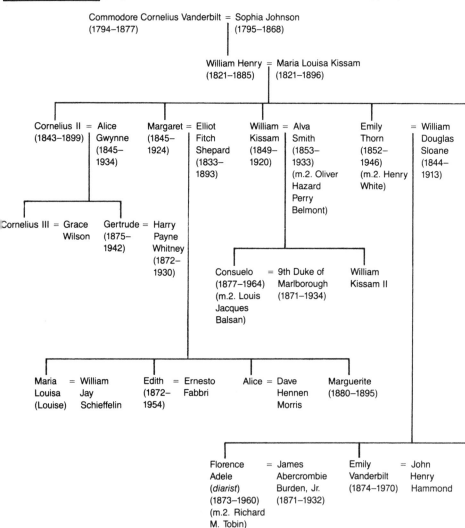

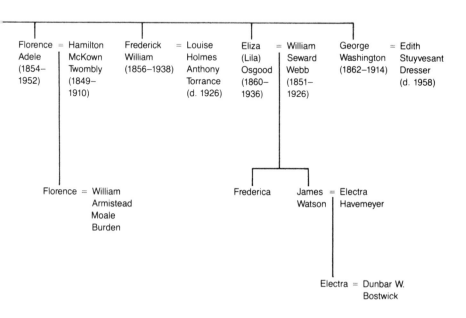

Florence Adele (1854–1952) = Hamilton McKown Twombly (1849–1910)

Frederick William (1856–1938) = Louise Holmes Anthony Torrance (d. 1926)

Eliza (Lila) Osgood (1860–1936) = William Seward Webb (1851–1926)

George Washington (1862–1914) = Edith Stuyvesant Dresser (d. 1958)

Florence = William Armistead Moale Burden

Frederica

James Watson = Electra Havemeyer

Electra = Dunbar W. Bostwick

Lila (1878–1934) = William Bradhurst Osgood Field

Malcolm Douglas (1885–1924)

Adele, painted by B. C. Porter, 1895.

1

Portrait of the Diarist
as a Young Woman

Florence Adele Sloane described herself to her diary, in the summer of 1893, at age nineteen, in the following fashion:

> I have an easy natural figure, because I have never worn anything tight or never in the least squeezed myself. I have a moderately small foot, and I suppose a very well-shaped leg; only no one ever sees that. . . . My eyes are black and my eyelashes long and my eyebrows thick. My hair is dark brown and brushed back off my forehead, with sometimes a little curl in the middle, and always done in a Psyche knot in the back. I suppose I am moderately graceful, and perhaps very much so on horseback; at least, so people tell me. But after this truthful picture I certainly cannot understand how people can look at me and tell me that I am beautiful.

Proceeding now to her personality, she writes that people call her clever, but she insists that any other girl with her education and travels would be the same. The real thing about herself, she surmises, is that she is "interesting"; she has plenty to talk about and cares for other people's points of view. On the debit side, she likes to flirt, and when she is not being "sympathetic," she is "cold and un-get-at-able," and no one knows what she thinks or feels. She concludes:

> There is my opinion of myself. It is *true*, seeing that there is no object of my making it otherwise. I have often thought, if I could remake myself, how different that self would be from what it is now!

In the previous year, just before Adele started the diary that she was to keep for three years, Ward McAllister published his famous list of the "Four Hundred" persons (actually nearer three hundred) purporting to represent the inner circle of New York society, limited, supposedly, to the number of guests that could be comfortably accommodated in Mrs. William Astor's ballroom. McAllister, a self-appointed court chamberlain to that indefatigable hostess, was the kind of fashionable ass that is taken up by idle women and despised by their husbands, and he was soon to be relegated to the windy alley of forgotten cotillion leaders, but if his list contained the name of a young unmarried woman, one could be sure that she had made her mark in the social world. And Adele Sloane's name appeared on his list, independently of those of her parents.

She used to say in later years that she had differed from many of her friends in that she had actually enjoyed the "gilded age." Mrs. Winthrop Chanler, a generation older than Adele, who had observed the same New York social scene at the same period, but from the more sophisticated viewpoint of a person raised in Rome with a literary and artistic family background, wrote that the Four Hundred "would have fled in a body from a painter, a musician or a clever Frenchman." To this older witness, McAllister's Gotham seemed a "flat and cold world," guilelessly proper and well behaved, but also "censorious and dull."

Not so to Adele. She saw the dances and the house parties and the yachting trips as Miranda in *The Tempest* sees the newcomers to her father's magic island:

> O, wonder!
> How many goodly creatures are there here!
> How beauteous mankind is! O brave new world,
> That has such people in't!

To which the more wordly-wise Mrs. Chanler might have replied, like Prospero:

> 'Tis new to thee.

Adele was not to keep her illusions forever, but one can't help being glad that she started with them. Like many who are blessed with that rare gift of a love of life, she looked around the scene that her parents presented to her in a generous mood. When one thinks of the paucity of happiness that was created by all the fantastic extravagance of that somewhat tarnished era, it is pleasant to think that at least one lively girl got a kick out of it.

Her parents wanted only good things for their three daughters. Her father was anxious that they should be cultivated, and cultivation in the 1890s meant Europe. Adele attended a small private girls' school in New York, from which she could be plucked at any time for a trip across the Atlantic. She learned to speak French, Italian, and some German, to play the piano, to recite poetry, and to recognize masterpieces of painting and sculpture in the museums and palaces of the great European capitals. History and philosophy were derived from courses in reading. Economics and science were no more required than cooking. A girl of fortune was brought up to be able to supervise a large household, to entertain guests, and to be passable in summer sports. If she could ride—and Adele was a brilliant equestrian—that was more than enough.

Everything for a girl, of course, pointed to marriage, and in that respect rich New Yorkers were less worldly than their European counterparts. The Sloanes naturally regarded a fortune in a suitor as at least some guarantee that he was not attracted solely by their daughter's, but a fortune was by no means a necessity. Character was the essential thing. An honest, ambitious, clean-cut young man without a penny to his

Adele's father, William Douglas Sloane, 1905.

name would have been preferable to a wealthy roué. Adele agreed. But she was ultimately to find herself vulnerable to non-wealthy roués.

The Sloanes had not left the high Presbyterian austerity of their native Scotland very far behind. Adele's grandfather William Sloane had been an apprentice weaver in Edinburgh who, in 1834, after his employer's failure to compensate him for inventing a new method of creating tapestry rugs, had emigrated to New York, where he and a brother, John, established a carpet business under the name of W. & J. Sloane. The store prospered and expanded into furniture and interior decoration; branches were established all across the country. William's sons took it over from their father on his death in 1879.

Adele's mother, Emily Vanderbilt Sloane (later White), in her twenties.

The Sloane sons were attractive, industrious, high-minded men; their reputation in the community was the finest. But a certain social stigma still attached to "retail" businesses. Livingstons and Van Rensselaers, in the middle of the last century, were not overanxious to give their daughters even to wealthy shopkeepers. One can imagine the motto they may have given the Sloanes: "From rugs to riches!" But the advance of the new fortunes, from whatever source, over the attenuated remnants of Dutch and British colonial society had, by the end of the Civil War, acquired the ineluctable force of a glacier. It was not necessary for the daughters of the newcomers to look for coronets or for their sons to seek out Stuyvesants. The best thing that a young man could do was marry for love in his own set, which is precisely what

Commodore Cornelius Vanderbilt, Adele's great-grandfather, painted by Eastman Johnson (a posthumous portrait).

William Douglas Sloane did in 1872. Viewing him, handsome and proud, buttoning the glove of his pretty, redheaded bride, Emily, in the Seymour Guy family painting of the Vanderbilts in their Fifth Avenue parlor, one feels that that young couple had the world before them.

Adele's father always maintained an interest in the family business. He served on the board of directors and sometimes as an officer. It was an American custom for the men to work, even if they didn't have to, which was a factor in making New York society different from that of London, Paris, or Rome. But the men did not have to work very hard. There was plenty of time for hunting, fishing, and golf on long weekends and in longer summers, and for extended trips to Europe and to the West.

The pattern of life that evolved for William and Emily Sloane was characteristic of their class. In the winter months they occupied No. 642 Fifth Avenue, the eastern half of the northern twin of the great brownstone cubes that Emily's father, William Henry Vanderbilt, had erected between Fifty-first and Fifty-second streets. In the summers they moved to Lenox, Massachusetts, a newly fashionable resort in the Berkshires, where they put up a vast rambling pile of shingle and brick, surrounded by broad lawns and gardens, called Elm Court. Spring or autumn was the time for Europe and the exiguous vacations granted to the great staff of maids, footmen, coachmen, and gardeners that kept the two establishments going.

The Sloanes were domestically minded. Emily was a small, kindly, conservative woman, of no great intellectual pretensions, who loved to play cards, travel, and be with her family. Her husband was a grave, handsome, dignified gentleman, with quiet humor and sound common sense, who spent much more time with his children than most fathers of his generation. But, as in many rich families of that era, the daughters fared better than the sons. They did not have to prove themselves "men" in a society where manhood was equated with making, rather than inheriting, money. The generation immediately following the founding father could, like the Sloane brothers, preserve their male image as aides and stewards to their sire, but the third generation found it more difficult.

The Sloane ancestry was hardly formidable, but Emily's grandfather Commodore Cornelius Vanderbilt loomed imposingly. The tall, imperial, frock-coated figure on the pedestal outside Grand Central Station might have been a source of pride to his female descendants, but it could be a crushing challenge to the males. William and Emily's son, Malcolm, became an alcoholic and died young. His story was to some extent repeated in the lives of his cousins, Elliott Shepard, Jr., and Reginald Vanderbilt.

2

The Yankee Medici

In 1873, the year of Adele's birth, her great-grandfather the Commodore was still very much alive and very much in control of both his fortune and family. He was a big, handsome old man, with a fine head of white hair, who had no pretensions to leadership of the social life of Manhattan. It was enough for him to be the Lord of the New York Central Railroad and the richest man in the nation. I suspect that he may have even exaggerated his rough manners and language in order to impress on people that he owed nothing to anybody but himself, and that, however grand they might deem themselves or their antecedents, they had to deal with the Commodore on his own terms. He bribed judges and whole legislatures; he hired gangs of toughs in his railroad wars; but at least he was a creative force. He covered the countryside with tracks and changed the face of America. He did not, like his opponents, Jay Gould and Jim Fisk, make his fortune simply out of the dishonest manipulation of securities.

He lived simply, by the standards of his day, except for one great splurging European trip abroad on his vast yacht, the *North Star*, which was then promptly converted to commercial service. But for all of his disdain of social life, he harbored the desire to create a dynasty. When he had decided at last that his elder son, William Henry, was the child to accomplish

The family of William Henry Vanderbilt, painted by Seymour Guy, 1873. *Left to right*: William Henry, Frederick, Maria (Mrs. William H.), George, Florence, William K., Lila, Margaret Shepard, Elliot Shepard, servant (in rear), Emily Sloane, servant (in rear), Alice (Mrs. Cornelius II), William D. Sloane (buttoning Emily's glove), Cornelius II.

this purpose, he bequeathed him a fortune of a hundred million dollars, a size unheard of in American probate history, and cut off his eight daughters and younger son with a scant quarter of a million apiece. They sued to break the will, but as they had little to go on besides their resentment, their happier brother was able to settle the case with a slight padding of their legacies.

William Henry had the personality and the good fortune of a competent caretaker. Between his father's death in 1877 and his own in 1885 he did not have to more than sit on his Central stock to have it double in value. He was a plain, simple

man, with none of the fire or color of his progenitor, but he
was much beloved by his sons and daughters, and far more in-
dulgent with them than the Commodore had ever been with
him. He is remembered most for his famous retort to a journalist: "The public be damned!" His granddaughter Adele in
later years used to insist that this remark had been taken out
of context; that what he had actually said was: "The public
be damned, I have my stockholders to consider." It was characteristic of her generation to believe that a corporate president's obligations, both legal and moral, were limited to his
shareholders, even when these were largely comprised of himself and his family.

William Henry compromised with his father's system of
primogeniture. He bequeathed ten millions to each of his four
daughters and two younger sons, and divided the residue between the two older, Cornelius II and William K., who received some eighty millions apiece. But there seems to have
been no dissent or dispute among the mutually devoted heirs;
there was plenty for all, and, more unusually, they all seemed
to recognize the fact. Of the two younger sons, George was
able to rear the greatest house of all, Biltmore, in Asheville,
North Carolina, while Frederick, like Fafner in *The Ring of
the Nibelungen*, sat on his gold so profitably that it grew in
half a century to equal an older brother's portion.

The eight children had not had to wait for their father's
death to start living in the style to which Vanderbilts rapidly
began to accustom the newspaper readers of their day. The
architect Richard Morris Hunt had already commenced his
long and profitable connection with the family by designing
for "Willie K.," at the northwest corner of Fifty-second
Street and Fifth Avenue, the splendid gray French Renaissance château, inspired by the house of Jacques Coeur at
Bourges, that had been the site of his wife Alva Vanderbilt's
ambitious fancy dress ball, cited by journalists as the first
great drive of the Vanderbilts for social recognition. And
Cornelius II had begun construction of the "Blois" château at

The Cornelius Vanderbilts' Newport house, The Breakers, 1899.

Fifty-seventh Street and Fifth Avenue that was ultimately to be the largest mansion in the city.

But now, with William Henry's death, the last lid was off, and all eight began to build. Hunt designed The Breakers and Marble House in Newport for Cornelius and Willie K., and Biltmore for George. Margaret Shepard commissioned a great pile in Scarborough, New York; Lila Webb and Emily Sloane erected shingle palaces in Shelburne, Vermont, and Lenox; Florence Twombly built Florham at Madison, New Jersey; Frederick set up a mausoleum of a country house at Hyde Park, New York—there seemed no end to it.

By 1893, when we shall make our first acquaintance with Adele's diary, her mother and her four maternal uncles and three maternal aunts had probably between them more beaux arts palazzi, more wide-ranging rural demesnes, more yachts, pleasure domes, greenhouses, and servants than any other group of siblings since those of Napoleon Bonaparte.

3

The Fourth Generation

The social life of the rich in the 1890s is just beginning to receive serious academic attention. It has traditionally been left to hacks who do their research in the society columns of old evening newspapers or in the books of other hacks. The scholar who would have gladly broken his back over the smallest purchase of Madame de Pompadour would have scorned to record the greatest of Alva Vanderbilt; the latter was too recent not to be still resented. But now this chapter of American sociological history is being given its proper niche. Anyone who has watched the long lines of tourists waiting to be admitted to even the smallest of Newport's "cottages" may have suspected that not all of them have come for the mere pleasure of daydreaming that they "dwell in marble halls." Some might be trying seriously to reconstruct a bygone era.

In the pages of Adele's diary we see this world from a fresh point of view: that of youth. The reader is at all times very much aware of the flotilla of her first cousins: Vanderbilts, Shepards, Webbs, Twomblys, Sloanes, many of them her exact contemporaries. They move in an amiable, chattering flock from Lenox to the Adirondacks in New York State to Beverly, on Boston's north shore, up to Bar Harbor in Maine, and down to Newport in Rhode Island and further down to Asheville in North Carolina. We see them cantering through the hills in the Berkshires on a crisp autumn day, riding a buckboard on the trails of Mount Desert island, watching a sunset from the deck of a steam yacht. They are intent on pleasure, eager to enjoy life, and yet at the same time curiously unspoiled, even naïve. One is sure that disillusionment lies in store for many of them—or is that only because one knows that in fact it did?

Some might try to read into the closeness of the cousinage the seeking of a strength in numbers against an older New York society still suspicious of the newly arrived Vanderbilts and Sloanes. Mrs. Seward Webb—Lila—once told Adele's daughter that it was because she had been the youngest daughter of William Henry Vanderbilt and the beneficiary of changing fashion that she had been able to marry into an old Knickerbocker family. But if the children of William Henry and grandchildren of the old Commodore had still a few social hurdles to take, most of Gotham must have smiled on the charming and strikingly handsome fourth generation. And they must have smiled radiantly back; they wanted to like and be liked, to love and be loved. When Consuelo Vanderbilt, the daughter of Willie K., married the ninth Duke of Marlborough, it was only in tearful submission to her ambitious mother's threats of suicide. She really wanted to marry Winthrop Rutherfurd, and he her.

If the social peaks had been scaled by the parents, the financial ones had been long topped by the grandparents. But unlike successful burghers across the Atlantic who sought to identify themselves with an aristocratic, *désoeuvré* society, their New York counterparts continued to work. Adele's Vanderbilt uncles went to their desks at New York Central; her father and Sloane uncles went to the store; Elliott Shepard plunged, disastrously as it turned out, in street cars; Hamilton Twombly made a fortune in mines. It was probably the continued orientation supplied by Wall Street that gave this society its peculiarly straitlaced quality. Men who work, even part time, cannot devote all of their energies to hunting women and animals, like the aristocrats in the fiction of Ouida, Anatole France, Marcel Proust, and Gabriele D'Annunzio.

It is also true, more regrettably, that they have less time for the arts, assuming, which is always a question, that they have the inclination. Walter Damrosch, from the music world, and Richard Harding Davis, an editor and journalist, are the only American representatives of the muses who appear in person in Adele's diary, at least on this side of the Atlantic—the first, to play Wagner for her mother's weekend guests in Lenox, and the second, because he was a glamorous reporter.

Adele had no poor relations, but she had some friends who were not rich. Beatrice Bend, who appears often in the diary, had to work for her living. Her father had been head of the Stock Exchange and she and her beautiful sister Amy had also been listed in Ward McAllister's Four Hundred, but George Bend had died in a bad market and his widow and daughters had become dependent on richer friends for trips and house parties, somewhat in the manner of Lily Bart in Edith Wharton's *The House of Mirth*. Beatrice, however, had a stronger character than Lily; she accepted a paid job as companion to the motherless young Dorothy Payne Whitney and ultimately (in early middle age) married the diplomat Henry Prather Fletcher and became ambassadress in Mexico, Belgium, and Italy. A poor girl did not have to end with an overdose of sleeping pills, like Lily. She could even, like Elsie de Wolfe, establish herself independently as an actress and decorator, but this was rare and considered rather too exotic. Beatrice's solution was the more accepted one.

Certainly, Adele did not have to resign herself to a middle-aged diplomat. She could afford romance. Love was to play a great role in her life, and it commenced, just before she started her diary, in the winter of 1892.

4

Enter Gifford Pinchot

It was in that season, at the age of eighteen, that Adele went down to Asheville to visit her favorite and youngest uncle, George Vanderbilt, still a bachelor, who was then in process of rearing his immense, fairy-tale French Renaissance château to dominate thirty thousand acres of wild mountainous scenery. In the easier atmosphere of that large masculine household, Adele fell in love with the glorious wilderness, the long rides through the forests, the outdoor life—and Gifford Pinchot.

He was eight years older than she, handsome, serious, utterly unlike any of the callow youths she had known thus far. He had dedicated himself, unusually for a young man of that era and of his background (his was also one of affluence), to the art and science of forestry and had undertaken for George Vanderbilt the first comprehensive forestry plan of the western hemisphere. It does not appear that he was ever in love with Adele, for nothing else would have stood in the way of their union. It seems probable (we have only her letters to him) that he regarded her in the amiable light of a charming young niece of his patron, to be joked with, even flirted with, but never to be taken too seriously. She, of course, could never introduce the topic of love. She had to wait, and, poor girl, she waited in vain.

Biltmore, George Vanderbilts' residence in Asheville, North Carolina.

When she returned to New York, she wrote him long, in-
genuous letters, in an amusing yet touching effort to convince
him that she was not just a giddy debutante, but a serious stu-
dent of philosophy and the environment. Here is her first:

> 642 Fifth Avenue, New York. March 28, 1892.
> My dear Mr. Pinchot,
>   This finds me in a flourishing condition of health,
> and I hope you are enjoying the same state of affairs.
> The usual stiff and formal way in which I am accus-
> tomed to write! To say I am Biltmore homesick and
> miss everything terribly would be silly, so I will
> merely imply it. I went to church with George[1] yes-
> terday, and we walked home afterward and rem-
> inisced on Biltmore. And then in the evening we
> looked at all the photos of the place and had little ec-
> static fits over each one, which the others didn't un-
> derstand at all. We both imagined you in a blissful
> frame of mind dining at Miss Houghteling's—the

[1] George Vanderbilt.

Clowning at Biltmore, 1893. *Left to right*: Walter R. Bacon, Emily Sloane, Adele with Gifford Pinchot seated before her, Mrs. Bacon, and George Vanderbilt.

very name sends shivers down my back—but no, honestly, I think she is perfectly lovely and so pretty. And in the morning I thought of you in that dear little Sunday School; didn't the children seem better for their three Sundays' contact with my gentle and subduing spirit?

And I—what did I do? Well, Friday night I went to the theater but not to see *The Foresters* as I had expected, but another play, *Colonel Carter of*

Cartersville, typically southern and consequently it made me terribly sad and out of spirits. The reaction of having to keep quiet and dignified and shut up indoors is frightful. Saturday evening I went to the Princeton Glee Club and actually talked! College talk most of the time, greatly to my own credit, I am sure. But I really feel as if I knew much more about college now. You have told me more than anyone else, although of course I don't repeat your stories.

This evening I go to the opera, and more forced quiet talk. "Did you have a nice time in the South?" "Oh yes! Perfectly lovely." "But I suppose you are glad to get home?" "No, I am afraid I can't say I am." "And how is your uncle's place?" I have already answered these questions about fifty times and don't suppose fifty more will make much difference. I think I would give anything I have to be down in Biltmore again. But, goodness, this is not what I had intended to write at all; this was to have been purely an instructive epistle, so I shall begin immediately.

[Here follow several pages about clouds, and what they are made of, to impress him with how much she has "boned up" on scientific matters. ED.]

The length, the abruptness and the general queerness of this letter will probably more than astonish you and make my age drop still a few years in your eyes, but I assure you that I intended to make it only a short epistle of dry facts from which I hoped you would derive benefit; as usual my pen has run away with me and the time too. But my intentions were only good, and although the contents may be the personification of idiocy and stupidness (I don't think that sounds quite right) remember that I have always said that "my exterior semblance does belie."

And now: "*Mon premier est le premier de son*

Biltmore, in Asheville, North Carolina, under construction, November 11, 1893.

espèce. Mon second n'a pas de second. Et mon tout —je ne puis vous le dire!![2]

> Very sincerely yours,
> Florence Adele Sloane

642 Fifth Avenue, New York. April 11, 1892.
My dear Mr. Pinchot,

Why am I like that rickety tumbledown house we saw one day at Biltmore? Because I am decidedly weak in the upper story and have rooms unfurnished.

[2] A conundrum: "My first is the first of its kind. My second has no second. My whole—I cannot tell you!!"

It is crazy of me to be writing again when there is absolutely nothing to write about. But haven't I always said that when I once began a thing I never liked to leave it off? And when it is a question of an intellectual mind to educate I will stop at nothing, not even lack of news? This is not in way of excuse, as I don't believe in excuses.

Your letter was most entertaining and, allow me to tell you, very well written and expressed. Thanks for your encouragement, although I wish to inform you that my ambition is not to be a teacher; if I can do no more than that, I will retire to a back seat. And even between us, *I* do not want to be the only teacher; you have got to tell me just as much as I tell you; it isn't such tremendous fun to give advice. The only book I have on your recommendation is the *Bab Ballads*, and I want the next one to be a little more edifying. As for being a genius, you know I don't believe in genius for women; as none of them have had it yet, *I* certainly will not be an exception. No, my life will be humdrum to a degree and compare equally with most lives. Delightful prospect, isn't it?

You see, I don't feel a bit like being funny today. I would like to have a nice sensible conversation. I won't say serious, because a serious talk goes with a serious face, and you don't think I can look that for three seconds at a time, although I have assured you that I can. As for the predicted change in me, everyone here seems to think it has already come, but they will change their minds when I get out of the city. It is only being shut up here that makes me horrid and cross, and the weather has been so warm that I feel more than ever as if I had come back here in the middle of summer. I went out riding before breakfast the other morning, all by myself. At least the groom started with me; I don't know when he got home, for I tore for half an hour until the poor horse was steaming, and then my heart smote me.

Adele's maternal grandmother, Maria Kissam Vanderbilt, painted by John
Singer Sargent, 1895.

I was in at Grandma's[3] on Friday with George and
Mr. Hunt, and she got disgusted with us. "Why
don't you all pack up and go back to Biltmore
again," she said, "instead of always grumbling here?"
Well, we are off tomorrow, thank heavens![4] I am so
excited about it; the trip will be perfect I am sure.
We probably won't get home before the second
week in June, and I may not get home at all if the
right cowboy comes along, with the right horses—
who knows?

When you get this I will be spinning across the
plains; it is just what I want now. I have the most
wild desire in me at present always to be on the rush.
Don't you sometimes feel as if you would suffocate
having to keep quiet? And in two weeks we expect
to be camping out in the Colorado Canyon, and then
I will have all my spirits back again. We are going to
have the same cook as George had in Biltmore, and I
shall most decidedly get him to make some more mo-
lasses candy, and I shall also most decidedly have
some confabs in the spacious car kitchen with him
about Biltmore, and perhaps even get his opinion of
you.

Your most kind, persevering and painstaking in-
structress, *qui peut dire avec plus de vérité que
jamais: c'est moi, i.e., un ange!!*[5] Also your sincere
friend and well-wisher (that's all!)—

F. Adele Sloane

Rough Point,[6] Newport. August 17, 1892.
My dear Mr. Pinchot,

I am sitting at my desk and looking idly out on the
ocean, and counting the stars, and wasting my time

[3] Mrs. William H. Vanderbilt.
[4] She was going West with her family.
[5] She explains the conundrum in her first letter—"Who can tell you with
more truth than ever: It is I, i.e. an angel!"
[6] Frederick Vanderbilt's house in Newport.

wondering what I shall do. Shall I write, or shan't I?
I want to, and still I don't. There is nothing to say,
and still there is so much. I am in one of these unde-
cided frames of mind when I would like someone to
come up and say "you must do this" or "you can't
do that." If you were here you would say "write,"
after common politeness, but way off in the mountains, when my letter comes, you will call it silly and
nonsensical. But I have started now, and for want of
anything better to do I shall continue. Downstairs
my aunt is having a big dinner party, and the music
and the laughter and talking are coming to me up
here. I was too tired to go down, and too lazy for
the exertion of talking to a lot of strangers. It is
lovely here with a cool breeze coming in and a smell
of the sea, and I am going to break my promise of
not sitting up late. I came to Newport quite unex-
pectedly yesterday, had no idea of it until two days
ago, when I decided to come with my mother as she
would have been quite alone. I was sorry to leave Bar
Harbor, very sorry. I never enjoyed my visit so
much there.[7]

I wish you could have stayed longer at Bar Harbor; it seemed even shorter than two days, for we
did not have many talks, and there were so many
things to talk about that one does not think of all in a
minute. But you are coming to Lenox now. Be sure
and let us know when. Anywhere about the fifteenth
of September or sooner or later, if more convenient.
I will get my saddle horse beautifully trained; she has
been ridden very little this summer, as I have my
pony and Father's horse to ride, and they are both
easier to ride than mine.

You can't imagine how dignified and grown up I
am here. This afternoon and yesterday afternoon at
polo I talked and smiled, was cordial and distant, nat-

7 Pinchot had been visiting George Vanderbilt there.

Elm Court, William D. Sloane's residence in Lenox, Massachusetts.

The Dining Room, Elm Court. (*Courtesy Lenox Library Association. Edwin Hale Lincoln, Photographer*)

The Parlor, Elm Court. (*Courtesy Lenox Library Association. Edwin Hale Lincoln, Photographer*)

The Conservatory, Elm Court. (*Courtesy Lenox Library Association. Edwin Hale Lincoln, Photographer*)

ural and reserved. You would have thought that I
was in my element and loved it, but I don't. I hate
the gossip of this place; I hate the formality, and sad
to say, I dislike a great many of the people. But
others again I like very much, and the whole thing is
fun for a little while. The polo match was most exciting yesterday afternoon; all the best players were
in it, and all Newport was there to look on. I am
only here until Saturday, so am rushing at a tremendous rate for these few days. I went all through Mrs.
Willie K's palace[8] this morning. No description can
possibly give one an idea of how marvelously beautiful it is. It is far ahead of any palace I have ever seen
abroad, far ahead of any I have ever dreamed of. It is
another monument to Mr. Hunt! However, the
whole thing is a perfect copy of a French palace of
the fifteenth century, so you can't bring that up to
me as a proof that architecture has not declined.
When you come to us in Lenox, there are a lot of
things that I shall read to you. For, after all, most of
my opinions have come from books. Experiences and
real things are what I want now. I often think how I
would like to go off all by myself, under a different
name, as a poor governess, only not really be poor
nor live with anyone, just have people think so. Then
I would travel, go everywhere, see what poverty,
sickness and sorrow really were, what misery and
crime meant. I have lived and seen only one side of
life, and merely read and imagined the other. And it
is difficult to understand and sympathize with what I
know so little about. Then again, I wonder which
feeling is uppermost in me, the one that makes me
want to help the class of people I talk of or the feeling of curiosity to know and understand what suffering is. There is so much selfishness connected with
everything we do. Why is it that that feeling of self
always seems to haunt one?

[8] Marble House.

As usual here I am scribbling along at this tremendous rate, and you are laughing at all these foolish
remarks; probably I will laugh one day too. But
when one is only beginning to realize what it means
to live, life seems very serious, and not to be laughed
and jested away. I probably do a needless amount of
thinking, but it will all amount to nothing, and I will
outgrow it and forget, and be none the worse and
none the better. It is very late, later than I had any
idea of. The music stopped long ago, and the lights
are all out, and everyone has gone home. What
would my mother say if she saw me still sitting here?
I must not any longer.

Finally, I have come to an end, and I can hear you
give a sigh of relief. You see, that strong-minded person wasn't here who should have told me that I could
not write, so you have had to go through all this rig-
marole.

Very sincerely yours,
Florence Adele Sloane

[But he didn't come to Lenox. He may have sensed that he
was getting in too deep and that it was kinder to stay away.
ED.]

Elm Court, Lenox. October 2, 1892.

Dear Mr. Pinchot,

At last the house is quiet and we are quite alone;
the house parties have broken up; everyone has left
and I have settled down finally to do some studying.
It has been nice having the different people here,
and I have enjoyed it, and we have all carried on and
been happy the livelong day. Only now I am glad to
be by myself. I am very sorry that you could not
come to us; I had so looked forward to those rides
we were to have taken, and in fact I was so sure of
them that I had even planned out where they were to
be and had ridden way over the hills so as to be
quite, quite sure of the roads. I have taken some very

long rides lately and have gone over into valleys
where I had never been before and which are beautiful beyond words. One week I rode over seventy
miles, twenty-six miles one day, eighteen the next
and ten and fifteen the next few days, and I hope to
keep it up all through this month. Mamma has just
gotten me a new polo pony. George said that he had
bought six new ones for Biltmore. What fun we will
have trying them next spring—that is, if we go.

It was so interesting the way you told me about
your adventure out camping, and I got just as excited
as I used to when you told me about things you did
at college. I told you that I had a perfect passion for
stories, and you must tell me some more the next
time I see you—whenever that will be, probably in a
crowded ballroom or at a reception. "How do you
do, Mr. Pinchot? I am so glad to see you! How long
are you going to be in New York? Oh, only until tomorrow! What a beautiful day it is, and doesn't Miss
Brown look well? You haven't met her? Dear me,
you must immediately; she is charming, you know,
quite charming, and they say Mr. Smith is desperately in love with her." Doesn't that sound like entertaining reception talk? What did I say to you last
year at Edith's tea?[9] I don't remember, but it seems
to me that it was nothing.

I have been to three little dances up here and that
is all, no dinners or anything else, and the only one
of the dances that I enjoyed was one where I managed to slip out of the ballroom and took a long
moonlight walk; that part of it was perfect.

I am glad to learn that Punch is flourishing, also
that you have a bigger horse for those long rides,
also that you have a little dog for company, besides
Lily, also that you are enjoying yourself. I haven't
said half I wanted to say, but I have been on a walk

[9] Adele's first cousin Edith Shepard.

of three hours this afternoon, and am just a little tired; besides, I ought to learn to condense what I write into a few pages instead of stringing it out in the number of sheets I generally do. I would like to send some messages to the little Sunday School children; only I am afraid they would be rather astonished, so I will close abruptly.

Very sincerely yours,
F. Adele Sloane

Just three months later she decided to embark on a journal. There would be references in it to Pinchot, some of them passionate, but the tone, in the end, would be different. Adele was not a girl to make herself a permanent willow cabin at any man's gate.

5

The Diary: January 1 to February 6, 1893

New York. Sunday, January 1, 1893.
"A happy New Year to everyone! To all the people I love, and to all the people who love me. May the ones I love have what they want, and the ones who love me what they want."

That is how Mr. [Worthington] Whitehouse told me to begin this journal, and I laughingly promised him I would. I wish all the first part of it would come true, all but the last line; that cannot be, any more than the wish Temple [Bowdoin] had, when he locked on my bracelet. Neither of these wishes will come true. I wish they could for others' sake, but not for mine. Beatrice [Bend] asked me the other day whom I thought I could be happier married to, Temple Bowdoin or Worthy Whitehouse. I didn't know then; I do now. I am sure with Mr. Whitehouse. I could not love either, and for that reason Mr. Whitehouse would make me the happier; he would not be nearly so exacting, nor so jealous. He would believe in

me absolutely and marry me because he loved me, and not because I loved him. But as I do not intend to marry either, I
don't see why I am writing this.

I am beginning this New Year the way I began last, namely,
in bed. I am so tired, that it is literally a physical impossibility
to get up; it makes me dizzy and faint. I have never known
what it was before to be so dead tired. It will take me two or
three days to get rested. Mr. Whitehouse was not able to go
to the theater with us last night. He was quite sick, he wrote
me, and terribly worried about me, afraid that I also had taken
cold from our long moonlight walk. "And although once
more I must repeat," he wrote, "yesterday afternoon and
night were the very happiest of my life, nothing could repay
me for having you ill. I shall think of nothing else until I return
to town." I should think we *would* all be tired out. It was
twelve hours of steady going from the time we arrived at the
Country Club Friday afternoon and went out for our walk at
five o'clock, till we got home from the second walk Saturday
morning at five o'clock. And that leaves out the walk I took
by myself Friday morning and the various other things I did
through the day.

Then yesterday was very busy too. I ought not to have
gone to the theater, but I wanted to be up at midnight and
hear the old year rung out and the New Year rung in, and I
could not have kept awake if I had stayed home. As it was, I
was up and opened the window wide, and heard the bells
chiming out. It was an ideal New Year's Eve like one reads of.
From my window I could see the Cathedral[1] spires looking
cold and white in the moonlight. The sky was clouded, but
not enough to hide the moon, and the snow was falling softly.
And through all the air was the sound of ringing bells. And as
I stood by the window the old year died, and the New Year
was born.

Saturday, January 14.

I had such a lovely evening yesterday. We had a little dinner

[1] St. Patrick's.

here first. I sat between Worthy and Creighton[2] and then later we went down to the Musical at the Common's. I sat back on the stairs where no one could see me, but where I could see everyone and hear the music to perfection. And it *was* perfection. The music couldn't have been lovelier, and Worthy was sitting by me, and, well, he could not have been lovelier either, and I felt almost as if I could not be happier, only it was a very quiet, sad sort of happiness.

It seems wrong to me to let him tell me always that he loves me so, and I told him so, but it does no good, and oh, it makes me so happy to have him love me this way, and he knows it, and though it may never come to anything, he will be thankful all his life, he told me, for having been able to make me happy. I am tired telling him how much harder he is making it for himself in the end, and he has made me promise not to speak of it any more. Over and over again I keep thinking of the music last night and his words of love. I was so excited I could almost believe I loved him, but the next second I am perfectly, perfectly sure I don't. But I could have cried when he had to go last night; he was going back to his mother in the country, and had to leave before it was over. I begged him not to, and then I was angry at myself for being so foolish and told him, of course, to go. And he held my hands and said: "Adele, darling, I love you so that I can't leave you; it is utter misery to go away." But why do I write things like this to be reread in a commonplace room, in an ordinary frame of mind, by broad daylight, when they were said with the sounds of soft music coming up to us, in the dull light of a staircase, and with feelings—I can't say how?

Sunday, January 22.

I am crazy to go away. I don't feel as if I could stand the city any longer. I have a desire for the country. Tomorrow I go to New Haven with Pauline Whitney.[3] It will be a change and I

[2] Creighton Webb, bachelor brother of Dr. Seward Webb, who married Adele's aunt Lila Vanderbilt.
[3] Daughter of William C. Whitney, later married Almeric Hugh Paget.

am glad; only I wish it were more of a quiet change. Every night there is to be a dance. I lead the Junior Cotillion and Promenade with Harry.[4] I suppose it will be fun. I am not going to any more dances when I come back here excepting the ones at the Burdens'[5] and Shepards',[6] and there are to be a lot of others. But I am tired of them. I am tired of a great many things, and there is a horrible fear in me that I may get tired of Worthy's love. Day after day I see him, and it is always the same thing, at dinners and dances and when he comes to see me, always the refrain: "I love you, love you, love you." It seems impossible to talk of anything else. I say nothing but sit quite still, sometimes looking at him, and sometimes looking far off, so far off that twice I frightened him [with] the thought that something had happened to me. I am happy, excitedly happy when he tells me how he loves me, but I do not think it ought to be. I am giving him nothing in return for all this, and it seems as if it were wasted. But I can't help it; he tells me it is a relief for him to talk; he must let some of the love in him out; it is not my fault because it is wasted; I can't give him what belongs to someone else, and he does not blame me. I am his love, his life, his soul. And then I feel utterly helpless. I don't understand myself. I am horribly lonely tonight.

I went out on such a jolly sleighing party last night. Jay Burden[7] asked me, and his mother chaperoned it. There were fifteen of us, and we drove for two hours in the Park and way outside. It was a beautiful night, no moon, but the snow is so white that it makes everything shine. I sat between Worthy and Mr. Perkins, but I talked very little; it was so lovely to think. I wonder if anyone will ever love me the way Worthy does. It struck me last night, though, that one cannot only be happy with love; there must be sympathy and understanding,

[4] Harry Payne Whitney, brother of Pauline, later married Gertrude Vanderbilt.
[5] Mr. and Mrs. James Abercrombie Burden.
[6] Elliott and Margaret Vanderbilt Shepard, Adele's uncle and aunt.
[7] The first appearance of James Abercrombie Burden, Jr., called Jay or J.

James A. Burden, Jr., B.A. Harvard, 1893.

and as much of it as there is of love. To a certain degree
Worthy understands me. He knows in a minute what I like
and what I don't like, what I approve of and what I disapprove of, and he never rubs me the wrong way. But I can't
help feeling that intellectually I know more than he knows,
have read more and thought infinitely more. We rarely if ever
discuss abstract subjects. He looks up to me a thousand times
more than I look up to him; in fact, I would be more sure of
my own judgment and opinions of a thing than of his. I know
my will is stronger; he could never make me do a thing. That
is what I mean by there not being sympathy between us. Perhaps it is the wrong word for it. But I want a person so much
stronger than I am, whom I could believe in absolutely and

entirely, and whose will and mind were stronger than mine. Creighton is like that, but his will is too strong; he would never give in to me. I don't want extremes.

LATER. I am more lonely than ever tonight. I had to say goodbye to Creighton this afternoon. He sails for St. Petersburg on Wednesday, and I won't see him again. I can't bear to think of it. He is always so lovely to me, and this afternoon he was lovelier than ever. We talked, talked, talked, and then he had to go. "You will kiss your Uncle Creighton before he goes, won't you, my little black pearl?" he asked. And I did. And he held my head in his hands and looked at me for a long while without talking, and then leaned down and kissed me, and neither of us said anything. No wonder I am so sad tonight. I can't say how I feel about Creighton. It is wonderful to have a man like that care for me and be my friend, and I am so thankful.

Sunday, January 29.

It was fun at New Haven and I enjoyed the novelty of it. Harry was perfectly lovely all the time; I admire him tremendously. We had a few long talks. I only wish there could have been more. We came home on Thursday, and I have been in the house ever since with a heavy cold. Yesterday Worthy came to see me. I don't think I ever dreamed or imagined such love as he has for me. I cannot get over the wonder of it. Sometimes he loses control over himself, and that frightens me; only I understand it and am so terribly sorry for him. Aunt Lila has asked him to go to Shelburne for all the time that I am there. I have never seen a man so blissfully happy over a thing. I am glad; only I wish it wasn't going to be for all the time. And if somebody else[8] comes there who has been asked, what will it be then? I can't think; he won't come, but if he does? I shall be too happy to live!

Sunday, February 5.

I have been reading a great deal lately, reading and thinking.

[8] Gifford Pinchot. He didn't come.

Coach and four at Lenox: Adele and Harry Payne Whitney in driver's seat.

There has been the old longing feeling of discontent in me. What am I doing with my life? What have all the days in this year been to me so far? Nothing, nothing. I have listened to the words of love of one man, and thought of them when he was not there. I am doing the same thing today. I will do it tomorrow. And what is it all for? Is there any good in it for me? Any good in it for him? No, it is all a horrible waste; it ought not to be. That is what my life is, a horrible waste. I ought not to say so, but I feel it now, feel it with a feeling that makes me mad. Oh! I wonder if anyone ever wanted to *do* something as much as I do. It is living in books that always makes me feel this way. I ought to have some work to do, some hard work, that would take my time and mind and everything else. I watch the people go by on the streets, and look at their faces and wonder what they are thinking of, what life has been to them, what their story has been. There is a sameness about them all, and yet a vast difference. When one is sad one's self, does one always find sadness and longing in other people's faces? There seems to be such a sadness and longing in all of them to me, all excepting the little children's faces, and they are happy and laughing; they do not know what life is.

I do not know why I should be sad, a mood perhaps, I have so many of them. I never can blame myself for not having warned [Worthy] enough, and telling him about the inevitable end that must come and bring such pain to both of us. He won't let me speak about it now, and he has made me promise to let him be happy those ten days in Shelburne. "I would give twenty years of my life to have these ten days of happiness." And I said yes. It will be a dangerous happiness. He loves me more every day, and what will it be after these ten days? It will be a dangerous happiness while it lasts.

I wish I wasn't so horribly sad today. I have just written a long letter to Pauline. Mrs. [William C.] Whitney is dying. I cannot think it; it seems so strange and terrible, she who was always so well and happy and full of life. My whole heart is going out to Pauline.

Monday, February 6.

Mrs. Whitney died yesterday. I have written to Pauline twice, and once to Harry. I can think of nothing else. If Pauline will only see me tomorrow, after the funeral, I am sure I could help her a little. I feel as if all the sympathy and pity in me was going out to her. I have been horribly sad all yesterday and today and cannot put my mind to anything. We have given up our dinner for tonight, a dinner of forty it was to have been, and I am not going to Aunt Maggie's[9] dance afterward. I don't feel as if I wanted to go anywhere. Worthy has just gone, and even he couldn't make me happy today. It is such a horribly helpless feeling to know that I can do nothing for the people I love who suffer. I cannot help Pauline, I can-

[9] Mrs. Miles S. Bromley (Margaret Kissam), sister of Adele's grandmother Mrs. William H. Vanderbilt.

not help Worthy, and I would give anything I had to be able
to.

The last time I saw Temple, which was weeks ago, he said
to me: "Do you think a man cares less because he never tells a
girl in words that he loves her? Cares less than the man who
tells her that every minute? Do you think his love is any the
less strong?" "No," I answered, "most decidedly, no. The
difference lies in their character, not in their love. For some
people it would be a relief to speak and let it out, almost a necessity. For others it would be hard and strained to speak of a
love they knew was not returned." "Yes," he said, "that is it,
and one could not talk commonplace talk afterward, when
this girl knew one's heart's secret, and what one was most
longing to say." That is so true. Worthy cannot talk small talk
to me.

6

Adele's Beaux

Worthington Whitehouse, to whom Adele so constantly refers in the diary, remains a rather shadowy figure. He was a member of a family well known in New York and Newport social circles, a punctilious and correct young man, who seems to have made a reputation as a cotillion leader. He never married and lived at the Knickerbocker Club. Adele did not take him seriously as a suitor, but she could never quite make up her mind to let him go. He was like a faithful dog, always there and always under control.

Creighton Webb was a very different proposition. To begin with, he belonged to the older generation. He was the brother of Adele's uncle-in-law, Dr. Seward Webb, who had married her aunt Lila Vanderbilt. The Webbs owned a great camp in the Adirondacks and Shelburne Farms on Lake Champlain, in both of which they gave elaborate and congenial house parties for their young nephews and nieces and their friends. The trip up on Dr. Webb's private railway train was only the beginning of a series of wonderful diversions: riding, hunting, fishing, camping, iceboating, tobogganing.

But Creighton Webb struck a less healthy note. There was something faintly sinister about him, something of the waxy, goatee-tugging villain of vaudeville, with a whiff of sulfur, and then, *puff*—it was just old Creighton again, up to his old

Shelburne Farms, Shelburne, Vermont, residence of Dr. and Mrs. Seward Webb.

tricks! He seems to have been quite serious about his brother's pretty niece, though she was twenty years younger than he. Indeed, it will become apparent in the diary that Uncle Seward himself was not indifferent to Adele's charms. But Creighton was not even thinkable as a husband. Mrs. Sloane told Adele that she would rather see her in her coffin than married to him. So that was that!

But it was nonetheless exciting, at nineteen, to have a sophisticated older man, a person taken seriously by one's family —even if they didn't like him—at one's feet. I can remember, at age twenty, in Bar Harbor, in the late 1930s, talking to Creighton Webb, then an ancient bachelor, partially senile, and finding him a quaint old relic. But there was still a dash, a flare about him, that helped one to put together the earlier figure that Mrs. Sloane had considered a threat to her daughter's happiness. He seemed the epitome of the "stage-door Johnny" of the mauve decade.

Adele and her first cousin Gertrude Vanderbilt Whitney in Renaissance costumes.

Harry Payne Whitney had a more complicated relationship with Adele. They were to remain the closest of friends until his death, in 1930, a friendship intensified by the underpinnings of romance. His father was William C. Whitney, Grover Cleveland's first Secretary of the Navy and a New York City traction-railway tycoon, and his mother, Flora Payne Whitney, William's first wife, who died in 1893. She was the sister of Colonel Oliver Payne, a possessive and jealous old bachelor and an early associate of John D. Rockefeller in the Standard Oil Company. Colonel Payne, apparently motivated by an obsessive devotion to his sister, took umbrage at his brother-in-law's remarriage, although it was to a socially acceptable woman and took place almost four years after Flora's death. He let it be known that his testamentary generosity to Whitney's four children would depend on their deciding between their father and him. Whitney's son Payne and daughter Pauline chose their uncle and were rewarded with one of America's greatest fortunes. Whitney's other son and daughter, Harry and Dorothy, stuck by their father and were limited to his much smaller but still ample estate. It is ironic that Colonel Payne, intending to disinherit Harry with a bauble, should have left him J. M. W. Turner's painting *Juliet and Her Nurse,* which Harry's daughter sold in 1980 for more than six million dollars.

Harry Whitney, everyone agreed, had charm—charm of character as well as of looks and manners. Adele was certainly not indifferent to this, and a nasty problem was created for her by a promise that his mother extracted from him on her deathbed. Flora Whitney, knowing that her son was idle, rich, handsome and beguiling, dreaded the prospect of leaving him to the clutches of the wrong woman and insisted that he give her his solemn word that he would wed Adele Sloane if she would ever have him.

Adele does not mention the episode in her diary, unless she tore it out later. The situation could have been used by Henry James in one of his stories. For how, after that happened, could Adele ever know if Harry really loved her? How, for

Adele and Gertrude Whitney in Turkish costumes.

that matter, could he ever know if *she* loved him? The young people promptly released each other. Harry, perhaps relieved at first, may then have begun to wonder if his mother had not had the right idea. Adele, in her turn, may have wondered if he would not have come to the point had his mother only left him alone. If poor Flora Whitney had wished to keep them apart, could she have contrived a better plan?

Harry married Adele's first cousin, Gertrude Vanderbilt, a year after Adele married James Burden. As the reader of B. H. Friedman's life of Gertrude, written with the full coop-eration of her descendants, will have learned, her marriage was not a happy one.[1] Both spouses were unfaithful. Gertrude, a brilliant woman and talented artist, could not long be content with a fashionable life of parties and sports, and Harry seems never to have found a satisfying occupation. But Adele man-aged to remain a close friend and confidant of both to the end.

[1] B. H. Friedman, *Gertrude Vanderbilt Whitney*. Garden City, N.Y.: Doubleday, 1978.

7

---◆◄►◄---

The Diary:
March 15 to May 1, 1893

New York. Wednesday, March 15, 1893.
We are all going to Europe in three days! I am too wild and
excited to speak. We have only just this second decided; in
fact Mamma didn't think of it until last night. It is perfect,
and I am so happy. We only expect to be gone six weeks.
Mamma has asked Edith [Shepard] to go with us, but I don't
know yet whether she can. I can think of nothing else; it is so
sudden. Perhaps Creighton will come to Paris to see us. Amy
and Mrs. Bend are going over the same day; poor Beatrice,
what will she do? I wish she were going as well. What will
Worthy say when I tell him this afternoon? I can't bear to
think. He will be so miserable. In his letter to me last night he
said: "I dread to think of the time when you go away. What
shall I do when I cannot look forward to seeing you? What
will become of the heavy days and heavy hours when I have
not my love to lift their heavy weight and turn them into sunshine? Ah me, I could not bear them all were it not that, even
then, I can have your homecoming to look forward to."

Adele with her first cousin Edith Shepard, 1894. Edith is in mourning for her father.

Hotel room in Paris, 1900.

Hôtel Vendôme, Paris. Monday, March 27.
The *Bourgogne* got in yesterday afternoon at 2:30, and we
came immediately on to Paris. The most terrible news reached
us in Havre. Uncle Elliott [Shepard] died very suddenly on
Friday. I don't know what I said or what I did when Papa
first told me. I couldn't believe it; even now none of us can.
Mamma didn't tell Edith until we arrived here. I wanted so
much for her to have at least one happy recollection of Paris
when she had been looking forward to it for so long. Today
has seemed perfectly interminable. I slept with Edith last

night, but neither of us went asleep until after two, and I was awake very early this morning. We have done nothing today excepting to order the few things necessary. Uncle Elliott's funeral is to be tomorrow. It will be so long before we hear any particulars. I feel tired and heartsick tonight. Amy Bend told me of her engagement to Lanfear Norrie this evening. These two lines keep running in my head all the time:

> A wedding and a funeral—a mourning and a festival
> And this hath now my heart.

In a certain way they are both alike, both terribly sad but the one with a happiness, the other with a bitterness.

Easter Sunday, April 2.

We went to Notre Dame early this morning. The service was so wonderfully beautiful. The sunlight came in in long rays of light through the stained glass windows in the chancel. The long wax tapers shone dimly through the incense around the altar. The little white choir boys sang out with all their soul, and the music from the two organs pealed through the cathedral vaults. The procession of priests and bishops with their golden crosses held up high walked slowly through the aisles, *l'archevêque de Paris* in their midst stopping every minute to bless the little children, held up for him to touch. To me it was very impressive, and I wanted to stay until the end of the service but we had to go to Dr. Morgan's church. The service was lovely there however, and Bishop Dorne preached a sermon I will not soon forget. We are beginning to go around sightseeing again now. Edith has not been in Paris since she was a little child. We are all quiet; we think things, rather than say them. There have been a lot of cablegrams from home, but we are longing for the letters; cables can say so little. They want Edith very much home on account of the will, but there is no one going whom she could go with, and it is impossible for us to get off yet. It has made our short stay here so different from what we had expected. The weather is perfect, and Paris is very bright and gay. Every time I come back here I like it better.

I have not heard from Mr. Whitehouse yet; it is strange that he did not write me by Wednesday's steamer, perhaps I will hear tomorrow. I had a long twelve-page letter from Temple Bowdoin. He walked from the Mission School with me that Sunday before we left, and then came in for over an hour. We had a lovely talk, and I felt we were going to be friends again as we used to be. When he heard that we were going abroad he wrote to me and then came to see me off on the steamer. On the spur of the moment Friday evening I wrote to him, asking him to take my Sunday School class. I told him I knew it would help him as it had helped me. This letter was in answer to that. He could not conscientiously take my class. And then he told me all the reasons. It was a lovely letter. "I have always felt," he writes, "almost since I first met you, that underneath the reserved exterior between us you understood and could sympathize with me more fully than one person in a thousand, and I have always felt an almost irresistible longing to make a confidant of you." In the end of the letter he says: "Perhaps I will explain to you one of these days why I did not come to see you more often during the winter. When I told you it was because I thought you did not want to see me, this was the truth, although you said you did not believe it. It was the truth, but only the partial truth." I sent him a long answer, almost all about religion. It was what I feel, and I think he will understand it.

Sunday, April 9.

We have been in Paris for two weeks, and every day has been more beautiful than the last. We went out to Fontainebleau on Thursday and spent the day. I had a letter from Creighton on Monday. He feels fearfully that he cannot come on to Paris, but he has too much work in St. Petersburg to be able conscientiously to leave. It would have been so lovely to have gone around with him here. Friday evening we went to the opera to hear *Romeo and Juliet.* We sat way upstairs so that no one could see us. Both the De Reszkes sang, and it was all perfect. It is so long since I have heard an opera.

The mails come twice a week but bring me no letter from

Mr. Whitehouse. I don't know why I should care, but I do, terribly. I begged him before I left to try and forget me, to try and not think of me at all. Perhaps that is what he is doing, and I ought to be glad, but I am not. I want him to love me; I want him to write to me his love letters. It may be wrong but I cannot help it.

LATER. His letter has come, and it has made me happy and sad, both. He has been very ill since I left, too ill to sit up for ten days, and all that time, he wrote: "I only lay and thought of my love, my life, my heart going farther and farther away from me over the sea." All his letter was just how he loved me and how he could not live without me, what the terrible loneliness of it all was. I wonder if anyone will ever write to me that way again, if anyone will ever love me that way.

I went to St-Sulpice with Mrs. Bend and Amy this morning, to hear the music. They say that it is the most wonderful organ and organist in Paris. What we heard was beautiful, but to me there is nothing impressive or appealing in the Catholic service; it is all form. I hate that constant bobbing up and down, the ringing of the bell, the people muttering prayers and staring around. It all seems insincere and untrue. Of course there are some things that I like. I love the custom of going into church at any time of the day, and kneeling for a little while to pray or think. It does me good to get that quiet from the noisy bustle of everyday life. We went to Notre Dame afterward. They were having a very large funeral service. It was interesting, and we stayed almost an hour.

Thursday, April 13.

Amy and I have just come back from our daily expedition in Rue Cambon. Every afternoon for the last six days we have gone around to Colombon's and gotten ice cream or chocolate and cake. It is too much fun, and no one knows about it. Of course, we ought to go with a chaperone, and that is why it is so exciting, for we are always scared to death that someone will come in who knows us. So far we have only seen French people, or English, and a few Americans whom we never laid eyes on [before]. Amy went to a dinner the other night, and the German baron who took her out was so *épris* after an hour that he could not leave her, begged to come and see her and various other things. Amy told him that she and I went to Colombon's, as it was quite the thing for American girls to go around alone. So I am in fear and trembling now that he will turn up. We met him on the corner of the street as we were coming home yesterday, and both had palpitations of the heart, I for Amy, and she for him. It seems perfectly ridiculous to think of her being married next month; she can't take care of herself, and she never can go around alone; she is a great deal too young and pretty.

Edith is going to leave us tomorrow and sails on Saturday for home. I feel dreadfully about it and wish I could go too. She has a very nice governess and on the whole is glad to go. Her mother wants her very much; none of the business can be attended to until she is home. Our short visit in Paris has been so different from what we expected, and now the ending is the worst of all. If only Edith could stay! I can't bear to have her go.

We spent Tuesday in Versailles. It was another perfect day, and the country looked beautiful. Almost one cannot be sad when the world is so lovely, and Paris seems all sunshine and happiness now. And why should we be sad? This Easter time coming with the spring and the flowers make me feel and know that there is a wonderful life in every plant and tree and living thing, even though a short time ago it was still and dead. How dreadful it must be for people who do not believe in the life to come; I don't see how they stand it.

Sunday, April 23.

I have been rereading my journal. How much sameness there is to it, all about the one thing. It gets horribly tiresome. How I wish I could meet some new people. It seems eternal ages since I have made any friends. I would like to go out in Paris and see a new society from what I have always had. I want to meet an entirely new set of people. I don't feel a bit like going home. I want to see my friends, but I don't want to go home. It will be just the same again, the same life and the same people. I hope I can accomplish something this summer; I ought to.

We have not had a drop of rain yet; the country is beginning to be in terrible need of it. It is wonderful to have such weather last. It has been very warm these last few days, almost uncomfortably so. We go to London on Friday.

I drove out to St-Germain Tuesday in Mr. Higgins' coach. Mr. Gregory asked me, and I had such a lovely afternoon. Monday night we went to the opera to see *Lohengrin* with [Ernest] Van Dyck in it. It was too wonderful for words. I suppose I have seen now the three greatest men in that part —Jean de Reszke, [Max] Alvary, and Van Dyck, each more wonderful than the last. I have also heard [Pablo de] Sarasate, the great violinist, and have been to the Théâtre Français. Several short plays were given at the latter; one, the most thrilling tragedy I have almost ever seen, called *Une Famille au temps de Luther*, the principal part taken by Mounet-Sully. I had never been before, and it was so enjoyable. We go to London on Friday. Every time I come to Paris I love it better and hate to leave it more.

I have had another long letter from Mr. Bowdoin. It was so much easier for him to write to me, he said, than it was to talk to me. My letter to him was perfect, he wrote, and had done him a world of good. "You always influence me for the good," he writes; "I remember perfectly that first time I met you at the Bends' dinner feeling elevated and stimulated by talking with you. The confidence and regard you showed by asking me to take your class has done me a world of good, and now in this last letter again you have given me a new impulse to exertion in the right direction." He told me he would be willing to trust me with anything.

It does one good to have someone believe entirely in you; it helps you. So often now I disbelieve in myself; I can't understand things at all. I get discouraged. For weeks at a time, almost, I am indifferent to religion, and each time it is harder to

Adele on horseback in Paris, 1900.

bring myself back to where I last stood. I would a great deal rather have disbelief and doubts and questionings than indifference; that is much the worse state to get into. In the first, your religion is alive; in the second, it becomes dead. It is just this religion that Temple thinks I have, and wants me to help him to have as he used to. Helping someone else may help me. God grant that it will!

I had a letter too from Creighton yesterday, asking me to give him some advice. "Strictly private," the letter was marked, "and not to be read to anyone." I couldn't imagine what he had to tell me. He might be recalled any minute, he said, under the new government. Had he better resign at once, or wait till he was called? It was outrageous to no sooner get him settled there than to want him back. If that were the case, I should resign at once, but I should find out very surely first. It may only be a mistake. He is so dreadfully lonely. It makes me sad every time I have a letter from him. He is the sort who needs friends and understanding and sympathy, none of which he gets there.

We had a cable from Edith this morning, saying she had arrived safely. It was so nice to hear. It seems much longer than a week since she left.

Hotel Bristol, London. Monday, May 1.

We have been here three days but I have not enjoyed it very much, because I have been feeling so wretchedly. Saturday, however, I did a little sightseeing, went to St. Paul's Cathedral, and then to the National Gallery. I remember everything perfectly; it does not seem as long as two years and a half since we were here. There was one picture in the gallery that I do not remember having noticed before and that had a most peculiar fascination for me. I could not take my eyes off it, and I have a wild desire now to see it again. It is a half-length portrait of Dante's Beatrice by [Dante Gabriel] Rossetti. She is sitting down, her head thrown backward, and gazing into space. I have never seen such an expression in a face; I think of it all the time. There is nothing except the opera which gives me more pleasure than pictures, or leaves such an impression on me. I wonder why. I haven't a single talent; I can't draw; I don't do anything. At one time I thought I could sing. I was crazy about it, and then I strained my voice, and for the last two or three years I have had a great deal of trouble with my throat, so all I hope is gone in that direction. One cannot cultivate a talent when one hasn't even the beginning of it; it is discouraging, and one cannot help but think how unevenly things are divided.

Saturday night Mr. Sellar gave us a small dinner at a club, and we went afterward to the theater to see a very funny play called *Charley's Aunt*. I have never seen a whole house in such gales of laughter. Mr. Sellar's stupid son, who visited us in Lenox two years ago, was there, but I scarcely said a word to him; he can only talk about horses and racing, and is so uninteresting, but the man who sat the other side of me at dinner, Mr. Denniston, and who was by me at the theater, was very nice and I liked him and talked to him the whole evening. I wish I could see him again. I am sure he thought I was queer. Half the time he looked amused, and half the time interested. He said English girls only talk about the weather and dances, and think it dreadful if the conversation gets any deeper. To-night I am going to dine with the [Robert] Bacons and Clarence Barker, and then go to see [Henry] Irving and Ellen Terry in *Thomas à Becket*.

8

Adele's Aunts and Uncles

Elliott Shepard, whose death Adele records from Paris, was the husband of her mother's eldest sister, Margaret Vanderbilt. He had been a strict Presbyterian who had not wanted to allow the municipal bus lines in which he invested to operate on Sundays. He was a hard, autocratic man, possessed of much worldly ambition; he wanted the great house that he had erected in Scarborough, New York, to be the seat of a dynasty. It is now the Sleepy Hollow Country Club.

Shepard, who dissipated all of his wife's money that was not tied up in trust, was not popular in the family. He told one of his daughters that her personal deformity was a punishment from God. One of his grandsons said to me: "I don't know if there's a hell, but if there is, Grandpa Shepard is surely in it." But Edith, his oldest daughter, who was sent home for the reading of the will (one wonders if there was anything left to bequeath) was Adele's closest friend as well as cousin. They had been presented to society together in a ball given by their Grandmother Vanderbilt in the picture gallery at 640 Fifth Avenue under the Meissonier battle scenes and Corot lakesides and Gérôme slave girls.

Of Adele's four Vanderbilt uncles, Cornelius, Willie K., Frederick, and George, the last named was her favorite. He

The Elliott Shepard house in Scarborough, N.Y.

was only ten years her senior, more like an older brother than an uncle, and his Asheville mansion, Biltmore, was to her the most romantic spot on earth. Besides, had he not produced Gifford Pinchot? And then, too, he was the only Vanderbilt with a serious interest in arts and letters.

"Uncle Corneil," the eldest uncle, was the very opposite of George. He was a severe, hardworking, conscientious man, of the highest principles, who, with his wife, Alice (Gwynne), managed to invest a life of outward display and triviality with the mournful air of duty rigorously performed. They gave parties because Vanderbilts were expected to give parties. Adele sometimes stayed with them in their Genoese palazzo, The Breakers, in Newport, but she told me once, after giving the matter careful consideration, that Aunt Alice had been "pompous." Her particular link with this branch of the family was Gertrude, who was as different from her parents as possi-

Mr. and Mrs. William Henry Vanderbilt (seated in center) with their family at Newport, 1884. All four sons and one daughter are depicted: Frederick, lounging on the step beneath his parents; Cornelius seated to the left of his mother; George (with his niece Consuelo) seated below Cornelius; and William K., cap in hand, leaning against the wall to the far right. William K.'s wife, Alva, with a black cravat, is seated in front on the steps, to the left, with Seward Webb, bearded. Lila Webb is holding the baby, Watson Webb, with Frederick's wife, Louise, standing on her left. The children to the far left are William K., Jr., and Frederica Webb.

ble. Yet even Gertrude, for all her Bohemian pretensions, had moments when she could draw herself up quite as stiffly as her mother.

Uncle Fred Vanderbilt and Aunt Lulu (Louise Anthony Torrance) appear in the diary only as sponsors of the dashing Freddy Beach, the rather fast gentleman of whom the Sloanes were so violently to disapprove. They had no children, which removed them from the noisy and numerous fourth generation.

Uncle Willie was the most charming of the Vanderbilt men.

On a private railroad car, 1902.

Adele used to say that, had he not been her uncle, she could have fallen in love with him. But as he and his fiery, imperious wife, Alva (Smith), were beginning to split apart at this time, she saw little of them. She did, however, visit Marble House, in Newport, when it was first opened and found it a "dream of beauty."

Of the three Vanderbilt aunts, Lila (Mrs. Seward Webb), so near to Adele in age that she called her simply "Lila," was the favorite, and Shelburne Farms, in Vermont, with its barn vast enough to house a polo match and its thousands of wooded acres on Lake Champlain, the place she liked most to visit after Biltmore. Aunt Margaret Shepard was as much loved by all the family as her husband had been disliked, but as she loses both a husband and child in the short span of the diary, she is somewhat muted in mourning. Aunt Florence (Mrs. Hamilton Twombly), who survived all of her siblings—she died in 1952, at ninety-eight—and became a kind of symbol to society columnists of the stately and inaccessible dowager, seems not to have been especially intimate with Adele, though the latter had been named for her—Florence Adele.

Adele saw less of her Sloane relatives than of the Vanderbilts; they were evidently not so cohesive a clan. But her uncle Henry Sloane, the most active of the brothers in extending the family store to other cities, and his lively wife, Jessie, were friends of the Webbs and saw Adele on visits to Shelburne. Jessie, as it unfortunately turned out, was too lively for her small, grave spouse, which brings us to the question of divorce, then happening for the first time in both the Sloane and Vanderbilt families.

Two of Adele's aunts-in-law, Alva Vanderbilt and Jessie Sloane, were divorced from her uncles, to be remarried to two brothers. Alva, after trumpeting her marital wrongs to all and casting off her husband for adultery (obtaining a settlement of ten million dollars, Marble House, and sole custody of the children), married Oliver H. P. Belmont, also divorced, a son of August, the German-Jewish banker, and continued, in Marble House, to dominate Newport society. Jessie, on the other hand, who made no secret of her passion for Perry Belmont, another son of August, abandoned her two daughters and husband and was cast out of respectable society. That doom, once decreed, was irreversible. Her daughters were brought up never to know or even to mention their female parent. The younger, who married a French nobleman, was surprised when he wanted to meet her mother. "In France," he explained, when she pointed out what enormity Jessie had committed, "society may reject the offender. The family never does."

I recall a sad tale that my mother told me. Walking as a young girl on Fifth Avenue with an aunt who had been mar-

Adele's mother, Emily Vanderbilt Sloane White, with seven great-grand-children, 1930.

ried to a brother of Henry Sloane, she recalled how sternly she had been checked from running to greet the lovely Mrs. Perry Belmont (whose gift of a brooch my mother was actually wearing) and having to witness the administering of the "cut direct."

Such were the principles of the day. The wronged party in a divorce suit did not lose caste. What Alva established—though it took a bit of doing—was that the *remarried* wronged party also should not lose caste. She had called on all

of her first husband's siblings at the time of the divorce to insist that they take her side. When the close Vanderbilt family
ties prevented this, she would not ask any of them to the wedding of her daughter Consuelo to the Duke of Marlborough.
Adele's close friendship with this beautiful and charming
cousin had to await a later period in their lives.

There were other ways of handling relatives who crossed
the line to the wrong side. Adele had a Sloane uncle of whom
she had never heard until his widow died at the age of ninety-
six. I remember reading of the death of a Mrs. Douglas Sloane
II in the New York *Times* in 1959 and showing her the item.
"Who could that be?" she asked, for the paper mentioned a
connection with the store. "I suggest it's your aunt." And it
turned out that I was correct. Adele's cousin John Sloane,
who knew the story, told me that his uncle Douglas had been
exiled to the West Coast as a young man and had been sup-
ported, but never mentioned again, by the family. What had
he done? Nobody knew.

9

The Diary:
May 12 to July 2, 1893

It has been such a sad homecoming to us, and oh, I feel so old
tonight, so old and tired and dreary! Something has gone out
of my life, and I can't quite understand it yet; it all hurts so.
This letter from Worthy came tonight; when I write it down
perhaps I will know it more, know what it means to me.

> My dear Miss Sloane: I am very glad to know that
> you have safely reached home again. I want once
> more to open the old subject, and then I shall not
> pain you by speaking of it again. After more suffer-
> ing, I think, than most men have, I have come to the
> only conclusion that to me seems possible. When I
> received your letter I realized the utter hopelessness
> of my love for you. I realized, too, the sweet
> kindness and gentleness of your treatment of me, but
> stronger, clearer than anything else, the hopelessness
> of my love. I have, I do, *worship* you. Yet I have lost
> you; the time of my sacrifice has come. If I am to re-
> tain my reason, I cannot see you. Will the time ever

come when I can see you, hear you, speak to you, without feeling that I cannot live without you? I know not, beloved. I have loved you, oh, so well. What *can* I do without you? Yet *I must*. And in these two last words you will see it all. They have been your words to me, more than once, and now the time has come when they must be mine also. I never cease thinking of you; that I *cannot* stop. My prayers, my hopes are with you. God bless and keep in His most holy care, my *lost love*, the best and loveliest woman God ever gave to man to love—

Worthington Whitehouse

No, I don't want to understand that is all over between us yet; I can't. He says he has suffered, but what am I doing now? Oh no, it is nothing to me, all this! Didn't I tell him not to love me? Didn't I tell him not to see me? And now what have I to complain about? Isn't it just as it should have been? No, it isn't! Why didn't he tell me this instead of writing it? It doesn't hurt nearly as much when a thing is told as when it is written. Why didn't he come to see me just once? Does he think my friendship means nothing, is nothing to him? That I can give it one minute and take it back the next? I have given it to him, a true, deep friendship; I can never take it all back. And then he tells me he must never see me; I am already only a thing of the past to him. How it stings, that bitter truth. A thing of the past! And soon his love, too, will be only a thing of the past. And still, why should he go on loving me? I am not giving him what he wants; he has wasted enough love. Throw the whole thing over and give it up! Yes, that is best. It is his affair, not mine; he suffers; I don't. Oh no, it is easy for me.

Why didn't he go, though, that first day when I told him to go? Why did he keep on seeing me and loving me? Until I gave him what was highest in me after my love, my friendship, and cared so much that I would do almost anything for him. He is forgetting his love, or has forgotten it; that is it. It is rather tiresome and monotonous to him; he must have something new. It is just how Creighton [Webb] told me men were, and I said I believed it, and yet in my heart of hearts I did not. But perhaps I am judging him too severely. Perhaps it has been hard for him to make this resolution. But no, he would have seen me once more and asked me again if there was no hope if he still loved me as he did at first. And how he used to tell me he dreaded the time when I should tell him I was tired of him and not to come and see me any more! I couldn't understand why he said it so often. "As if we could ever get tired of one's friends," I used to answer. "What do you take me for?" I see now that he judged me from himself. I suppose we must all have our illusions broken and dreams taken away some time. It is hard first, so hard that one rebels against it and cries out with the pain, but in the end one gets used to it.

It is funny how he made me solemnly promise never to write to him that he should not come to see me; he would not live if I did. Oh, a great many things are funny, and they are all very fresh in my mind because I read all my journal over the last Sunday in London. I wrote to him tonight; it was better to have it over with. I said I supposed it was all for the best; only I thought it would have been better if he had told me what he wanted to say instead of writing it. I thanked him for his love; it had meant so much to me. It will be hard when I see him again; I don't want to think of it. I feel like going into shrieks of laughter and then crying my heart out. It has done me a little good to write; I could not keep it all to myself, and I could still less speak to anyone about it. A year ago today we were in Monterey; my heart was full with an unspeakable longing then. It is a hundred times as full tonight with that longing intensified.

Saturday, May 13.

It rained today, so I could not go to the country with Edith as we had at first intended to. I am sorry, for I know it would have done me good. I took a long walk in the rain this afternoon, and I am quite quiet this evening. I only slept a few hours last night, and all today there has been such a horrible emptiness in me, as if I had lost something or someone. It is all gone, and it is right that it should be, but oh how I want it again, how I want to see him! I don't love Worthy. I could never marry him. But now, to have it all stop at once, his letters and everything—if it could only have come gradually! I have thought of it so much and gone over all the reasoning he must have, before he wrote me the letter. He must have gotten mine from Paris three weeks ago. I begged him in it again to try and get over his love for me and forget it. "Try and remember," I wrote, "that I can never make you happy." And he *has* remembered it and is determined to forget. Perhaps I ought to admire him for it, for it must have meant a great deal to him, but somehow I don't. If he had only seen me *once* before deciding. If I were a man I would have acted so differently. I hope I will not see him now for a long, long while. Time does so much toward the taking away of the hurt and bitterness of a thing.

Mr. Crosby came to see me today, but they told him I was out. I think I will lose all my friends now and have to begin afresh. Temple Bowdoin was called away suddenly to Chicago; his father wrote me of it and that he would not be able to come and see me. I was so surprised to get the note. Temple had asked him to write it, for he was so hurried the last minutes.

We expect to go to Chicago a week from Monday. I shall be so glad to get out of the city. Today is the first day of rain we have had since we left America eight weeks ago. We had a few showers on the sea, but they did not last long. The trip back was not a very good one; we had very rough weather the first three days, but fortunately I felt perfectly well all the time, quite a contrast from what I was going over.

Sunday, May 14.

Amy Bend has broken off her engagement to [Lanfear] Norrie! Mrs. Bend told it to us today. It was all a mistake. Amy ought never have given him her word. She never loved him,

Sloanes and Bends, 1894. *Back row (left to right)*: William Douglas Sloane, Beatrice Bend, Amy Bend, Emily Sloane, George Bend. *Middle row*: Adele, Mrs. Sloane, Mrs. Bend. *Front row*: Lila Sloane, Malcolm Sloane.

and she has not been happy since she was engaged to him. I can't understand why she announced it. I saw so much of her in Paris, and from the first I knew she did not care for him, and was only going to marry him because he could give her everything she wanted and because it pleased her father and mother. But all along it seemed wrong to me and such an injustice to the man. And now she has been home a week and everyone has seen them together and congratulated them—and then to break it; it seems so wrong and hard for him. I blame Amy [Bend]; she ought to have thought more, and yet for her sake I am glad it is all over, but I don't want to see her quite yet. I think an engagement ought to be almost as sacred a thing as a marriage. When you have once given your word to a man, it ought to be final and irrevocable. You ought to know your mind beforehand so well that nothing can change it. After a man asked me to marry him, I would want to wait two or three weeks before giving my last answer. I could tell him that I loved him and know what the promise would be, but not give the promise until I knew nothing on earth could make me take it back.

Tuesday, May 16.

I have just come back from Scarborough with Edith [Shepard] and I found this note waiting for me. It has all changed and I am afraid to think how glad I am.

> May I come to see you? Forgive me for my letter and in mercy grant that I may come to you at any time you will appoint. It is so much better to do as you say in your blessed letter. I *cannot* lose you entirely when I may retain even a little of your friendship. Even this means more to me than could anything else in this world. And we can be *friends*— please God—until you care for someone else. After I wrote you I was ill at home for two days. Your letter was forwarded from here and I only received it this morning when it was reforwarded to me. Forgive me for writing that letter. I sometimes think that I hardly know what I am doing. I have thought so long and so much of one thing. Forgive me, and though I may never be anything else to you, give me the blessing of your friendship, and let me come to see you. Yours only and always, Worthington.

So all my bitter hard thoughts that first day were wrong! They have not been so lately, only sad, and almost I was beginning to think it was best what he had written to me. But

Adele, in the mid-1890s.

now I cannot tell him not to come. Sooner or later we must meet, and it will be so hard for both of us, after what has passed. Is it not far better for us to talk together quietly here for a little while? I am going away on Monday, so it can be a goodbye with all summer in between, and then the next meeting need not be constrained. It is not as if he were going away, or I never were going to see him again; then I would not think of his coming here. But it is inevitable that we should meet, and why not now? These are my unselfish reasons, but the selfish ones are far more. I care for him so much that I do not feel as if I could give him up. I must have him for a friend. We will not talk of love; I will tell him that, and then after a while it may all come to an end gradually. It was the suddenness that hurt me so. I have written him to come tomorrow afternoon. Have I done wrong? Oh, God forgive me if I have, and do not let him suffer for it!

Sunday, May 21.

I have just had a long, long talk with Temple [Bowdoin]— such a nice talk. He makes me feel that I have helped him, and it is so good to have a person believe in you. He asked me this afternoon if there was no hope at all for him, whether he had as even a chance as any other man of winning me. "As even," I answered, "but just as poor, so please don't try and hope." He spoke to me a good deal about it, all in a quiet way. "Perhaps," he said, "you do not think I love you, because I speak in such a calm way about it. But it is quite different; only it is no use talking to you about it; it won't do you any good, and it will only make it harder for me. If you tell me there is no hope I want to try and forget it; I have been so unhappy once, I cannot go through all that suffering again. But I will see you; I want to see you; I want to talk to you, and I want to write to you; I can't give up everything." When he said goodbye to me, he told me that I had been perfect to him. "I can't quite think yet that there is no hope," he said. "I wish you would write it to me in a little while when I am away from you; it will seem more real then, and I will try and understand it."

I will not say I am sorry for him, because it means so much more than that. When a man has been unhappy once, I don't see why he can't be happy the second time. Temple was engaged four years ago to May Webb. He told me about it today; only he did not mention her name; perhaps he did not know that I knew it. He was engaged to her for eight months; then Frank Webb came along, fell in love with her and she with him, and in three weeks they were engaged. It seems so horribly wrong to me, a thing like that. If a man loves a girl and makes her love him enough to promise to marry him, that promise ought to be sacred. If another man came along and loved her too, and she felt herself weak enough to care for him, she ought to tell him to go away and never see her; if he had any sense of honor he would go away. And she would soon forget, having had little time to think. It is pure selfishness to break with one man and ruin his happiness because, perchance, another man could make her a trifle happier. It had taken until last year for Temple to get over it, he told me, and it had made him different, and now he loved me, and would go on loving me a great deal more if I gave him the least tiny hope. He does not love me the way Worthy does, but it means a great deal to him, more, I know, than he tells me.

Worthy has been to me twice, and oh, I have been so glad and he was happy too, and he wrote that he would be to me "the truest friend God ever gave a woman"! We talked together and I told him things to read this summer, and it was so lovely to know that we were really friends. Only it will not last after I have given my heart to another man. But neither of us is going to think of that. How few people would understand that I can care for Worthy and still be in love with someone else,[1] but it is not as if that someone else loved me; then I would need no other love in the world.

These last two days I have been very busy with my Mission School children. Friday I took the boys up to the Metropolitan Museum and explained to them all about the Egyptian mummies and the Greek temples and other things; they

[1] Gifford Pinchot, of course.

seemed so interested. Afterward we went to a place and got ice cream and cake. Yesterday Emily[2] and I had our girls together, twenty-eight in all. They had ice cream and cake here first, then we took them out in two park wagons for an hour's drive. I am so interested in all the children. People do not know what they miss by not having a child's love.

We go to Chicago tomorrow. I am glad to leave the city. I want to accomplish a lot this summer. Lately I have been reading a good deal in Browning, and the more I read the more I understand, and oh, he does help me so much! It is only people who don't try to understand him, who say he can't be understood.

Auditorium Hotel, Chicago. Wednesday, May 24.

We arrived here yesterday at eleven o'clock in the morning, but to me it seems as if we had already been here for days, we have seen so much and accomplished so much. Immediately after luncheon yesterday, we all started out for the Fair Grounds.[3] You do not get a very good view of the buildings until you are right in the grounds, and then they suddenly appear to you in all their beauty and grandeur. Everyone says that it is impossible to describe the impression they first make on you, and everyone will have to go on saying that. I felt the same as I did when we arrived in Granada that moonlight night, three years ago, and drove through the dimly lighted streets of the city, and then up the hill through the tall trees to the Alhambra. It is a feeling one cannot tell of but which one never forgets.

The first thing we did was to get into a steam launch and go through all the lagoons so as to have a good idea of the buildings and see how they are placed. It is truly what one should call "the Dream City"; it is too ideally beautiful to be real. When we went into the principal lagoon, the Court of Honor, I actually stood up in the boat and almost screamed with wonder and surprise at the marvelous beauty of the

[2] Adele's younger sister.
[3] The Columbian Exposition, a World's Fair, was held in Chicago from May to October, 1893.

scene. On one end, the Administration Building with its high gilded dome; below, the Fountain of Neptune sending its waters into the lagoon. Opposite, on the other end, the graceful Corinthian columns of the peristyle, through which may be seen the lake stretching far away in the distance. On one side, the Agricultural Building; on the other, Manufacture and Liberal Arts. There is perfect symmetry in the plan and perfect beauty. We went all around by the Government Building, the Art Building, which is one of the loveliest of any, and then back to the Woman's Building, which is the first we went into. None of the exhibits are yet fully in place; in fact some of them are not arranged at all. We spent all afternoon wandering around, and then came back here for dinner, and afterward went to the theater.

This morning we started early. Mr. Miller took Emily and myself, and I never had a more interesting time. First of all we went to the Agricultural Building, then to the Convent of Rábida where Columbus used to go. It was the exact reproduction of the old convent, and we walked through all the little cells. Then we went to the Administration Building, Transportation, the Horticultural, and the Fisheries. For luncheon we went out to the Midway Pleasance and the German Village. It was just like being in a café in Germany. The waiters were German. There were two German military bands, and the people came in and sat around the tables and drank beer.

Afterward we had such fun going around to the different theaters. We went into an Egyptian temple and saw a most peculiar dance. Quite a pretty Egyptian girl was dancing, and she seemed to be moving every muscle in her body. It was very slow, and there was not much dancing with the feet; it was just a slow rhythmic motion of the whole body. After that we went to the Algerian theater. I had heard of that sort of dancing before, but never seen it. It is very strange. I wish I could have seen it all; only it was rather embarrassing sitting next to Mr. Miller. It is called *la danse au ventre*. The women begin when they are tiny children to train themselves. To a certain degree it is disgusting, but I could not help being interested.

After that we went to the Chinese theater. There a very funny play was being given, at least funny to us, because we could not understand anything, and the music was so queer; very ugly, I thought, but a Chinaman told us he thought it was beautiful and that *our* music was loud and dreadful! It shows how one's tastes are made by habit. Altogether the theaters were a delightful success. We went into several other places, and then came home.

Thursday, May 25.

Last evening we dined at the Richelieu Restaurant. I saw Mr. Pinchot there, and he spoke to me for a few minutes. He had been in New York all the week before. I thought perhaps that he was, but I knew he would not come to see me. I probably will not see him again; we only stay here until Monday, and one never comes across anyone one knows in the Fair Grounds, they are so enormous. I had a letter from Worthy yesterday and it made me happy. I cannot compare those two men; they are so different. One has everything a man ought to have, at least the things the man I dreamed of had, and the other—well, the other has a great many things: a perfect love, a very unselfish nature, and he is so considerate and thoughtful. But that is not enough; I want so much more.

Today we did a lot at the grounds. Spent the entire morning in the Art Gallery. Outside it is the most beautiful building of any, and inside some of the collections are very good. We took luncheon again in the little German Village and then went to some of the things in the Pleasance, the Bedouin Village, and the little house in Damascus. In the afternoon we went to the Transportation Building again and saw it thoroughly, and then to the Mining Building and through the Horticultural.

Saturday, May 27.

This is our last day for seeing the Fair. I wish we had another

Signatures on "calling cards."

week at least. The more one sees, the more one finds what
there is to see. The Manufacture and Liberal Arts Building
took us all yesterday morning to see and part of the afternoon. It covers forty-four acres of ground, and every avail-
able space is filled. The French exhibition is perfectly beautiful, also the German and Austrian. Everything from Russia is
behindhand. I am so disappointed because they said it was
going to be so rich. Everything in the Machine Building is
most interesting. We saw how materials were made, ribbons,
and all sorts of inventions. I went again to the Art Gallery and
saw the United States Collection, which is very good. We also

went to the Esquimaux village and spoke to the little Esquimaux children.

After luncheon we went to the Forestry Building. I wish I
could have seen everything in that, but the others were not so
interested. Very few things were in order. I saw the North
Carolina exhibition, which was just being arranged. Mr. Pinchot has had everything to do with that.

Thursday night we went out to the Fair and saw the illumi-
nation of the grounds. It rained hard most of the time, but at
least it was much better than not seeing it at all. We went in
an electric launch with the Bends. The principal lagoon was
perfectly beautiful and the whole Administration Building
was a blaze of light.

Sunday, May 28.

It is too bad that he[4] had to meet me here. Now I feel as if I
must see him again. It is maddening to know that he is so near
and yet that I cannot meet him. All the time in the Fair
Grounds I am looking and hoping to see him, and I was so excited last night because I thought he would be at the Richelieu
Restaurant, but Mrs. Pinchot was alone at a table, and he did
not come at all. I will never see him! I can't stand it, since he
knows how I feel. I tell Beatrice everything but that. She is so
sympathetic.

Yesterday I did a great deal at the Fair, and then said goodbye to it. I want to come back in the fall, but I am afraid
there is very little chance of it. In the morning we did a number of state buildings: Massachusetts, New York, and Con-
necticut; then Germany, France, and England. The last was
lovely. I know so much more what I like and what I don't
like now than I used to, and why I do—I mean in architecture. Studying Viollet-le-Duc has helped me so much. He
makes one understand things. We went on top of the Manu-
facturer's Building and saw the whole view of the grounds.
We had luncheon in the Vienna Café, and then went to the
Cairo Street, which was only opened yesterday. It is the best

[4] Gifford Pinchot.

street of any, and I was fascinated with it. Such a funny procession passed through while we were there. Egyptian men,
women, and children, some riding on donkeys, some on
camels, and singing strange songs. It gives one such a funny
feeling to see these weird performances in this country. We
went to the Moorish Palace afterward and then back to the
main grounds. I went through the lagoons again, stopped a little while at the Administration Building to listen to the music,
looked in the Music Hall, and went through the Electricity
Building. We drove home on the coach.

LATER. His card has just been brought to me! "Shall this
gentleman be shown upstairs?" And I answered distinctly
"yes," and then waited and waited, but he did not come. I feel
as if I must cry my heart out. Did they tell him wrong? Or
did he only leave his card? All this afternoon I stayed here,
hoping he would come. Oh, God, am I never to see him? I
have prayed so much today, and for a little while I thought
my prayer was answered.

Elm Court, Lenox. Sunday, June 4.

This afternoon I have been down alone in our little house in
the woods.[5] It was so quiet there and so perfect. I felt almost as
if I were hundreds of miles away from anyone. There was not
a sound excepting the low, moaning sigh which the wind makes
through the pines. The birds did not sing, for the sky was
heavy with clouds, and every now and then a far away rum-
ble of thunder was heard. I wrote my letter to Temple Bowdoin, the one he made me promise to write, and then I read a
little. I wish I could have stayed down longer; it is just the
sort of an afternoon I love, quite alone by myself.

I had certainly a much better sermon this afternoon than
this morning. I am quite happy in the country again; it is very
beautiful now. The season is behind here so we are enjoying
the full benefit of the apple blossoms and the lilacs, and the
trees still have that fresh greenness one always sees in the early
spring. I have been very quiet so far, resting from the excite-

[5] Cozy Cot, a playhouse at Elm Court.

ment of last week in Chicago. My room looks so pretty; I
have it to myself this year. Emily's bed and bureau are taken
out, and in their place I have put the sofa and bookcase. Half
of the room is my bedroom, and the other half, sitting room. I
have all my favorite Brown photographs hung on the wall, at
least a great many of them. Over my bed is the picture of
Sleep sending her child Dreams into the world, and, where I
can always see it, is Dante Rossetti's *Beata Beatrice,* the one I
loved so in the National Gallery. Over the bureau are
[Adolphe] Bouguereau's two Madonnas: *La Vierge Con-
solatrice* and the one with the angels, and between them *Les
Illusions Perdues,* which I have always loved. Over my desk is
the beautiful *Saint John* of Carlo Dolci. His head is enough to
inspire anyone. I could not love pictures more than I do.

Last Sunday in Chicago I wrote to Harry [Whitney],
Alonzo [Potter], and J [Burden] asking them to come here
the third of July for a week. The two last accepted immediately, but I have not heard from Harry. I am afraid he will
not come. We would have such fun together, and no end of
exciting sprees.

I saw Mr. Pinchot that Sunday evening, but only for a pass-
ing bow as he was taking his mother into dinner. It made me
angry first, that distant bow, as if he had never spoken to me
in his life. I was sorry and horribly sad. The next day in the
train,[6] without thinking and on the spur of the moment, I
wrote to him. It was foolish, and I am mad to do such things
but I did not think of anything but my longing to write, and I
mailed it at a station on the road so there was no chance of
taking it back, when I realized what I had done. But, strange
to say, I did not regret it; it was the most tremendous relief
for me to write, and it made me happy. It was very short. Almost I can remember now what I said:

> Dear Mr. Pinchot: I was sorry not to see you yester-
> day. It is so long since you have talked to me; almost
> I feel as if we were getting to be absolute strangers,
> and after I went . . . [A page is here torn out of the
> diary.]

[6] From Chicago to New York.

He told me how busy he was going to be this summer, how he had never had so much to do and so little time to do it in. Then he said goodbye until next winter. Mamma said the other day she would ask him up here in September, but it will be useless; he cannot come.

I have ridden every day this week and have been very happy. My pony is so sweet. I heard dreadful stories about him first; how he pulled and reared and was generally unmanageable, but he has been as quiet as a kitten with me. Half the grooms do not understand horses, and naturally if they pull and tug at a horse's mouth, they make him rear and plunge. I have tied the curb rein and ridden him with a light snaffle. It was perfect bliss to be on horseback again; I do not believe anyone cares for it more than I do. The days have all been beautiful, sometimes warm and then again getting cooler.

I heard from Worthy a little while ago. His stepfather has just died. I wish he did not have so much trouble. I have not written him since. Perhaps I will go down to Cozy Cot this afternoon like last Sunday and write to him there.

LATER. I was sitting in my armchair by the window last evening, watching, as I do every day, the sunset. It was so wonderfully beautiful. The deep crimson red spread all over the west, fading into pink and joining the deep blue sky. And the white clouds made quite golden, and the nearer they were to the sun the brighter and more golden they grew, till they seemed almost a part of the sun itself, and the little clouds further back seemed quite pale in contrast, till finally they only borrowed their color from the other clouds, and still further in the east lost it altogether, till on the horizon they were quite dark. And the thought came to me of how it was with us here. The nearer we live to God and in His great love, the brighter we are, and the more we reflect the image of the dear Christ who taught us what God is. The farther away we are, the dimmer we grow, till finally there is no light at all. And I wondered how near I was, whether I had the real gold in me, or only the reflections of the gold. It is not gone, I am sure of that, but is it very bright?

I wrote out my mental photograph in Beatrice's book a little while ago, and several of the questions made me think a good deal. One was: What is your aim in life? And I answered: "To make my life worth the living." That means a great deal, but there is no especial aim in it. I am always saying I want to do something, but what? What is the something I want to do? I don't know. That is the true answer. I want to live up to my motto, "To thine own self be true," but half the time I am not. I say things I don't mean; I do things I don't want to do. Sometimes I think it is impossible to be absolutely true in society, with the false note going all through it. But then again I know that it is not, for the trueness does not begin with outside people; it begins with oneself, and when one is true to oneself, then one must be true to everyone.

"Don't fight over the little trivial things and conventionalities and worldly questions, the dainties of life; they are not worth the while. But fight and struggle over the few great truths and principles, the bread by which we live." That is what Mr. Grosvenor said in his sermon this morning. And I thought the same with religion. Why argue and dispute over the little questions that we cannot think alike in, when there are the few fundamental truths we all believe in? The Bible is so broad that it does not lay down laws that we must think this or that, and not the other. These are not the truths we live by; it is only the few great laws that everyone, whether they want to or not, must know to be true and must live by.

Mamma asked Dr. [David] Greer to come up here, and I am so disappointed that he could not come. I have gone to his church[7] entirely this winter; it made Mamma feel badly, but she understood it. Everything that Dr. Greer says helps me and encourages me, and I answer "yes" to it all. The last sermon he preached was: "And because I live, ye shall live also," and he gave such an easy illustration to it. "Cannot you picture to yourself," he said, "in this springtime, the little seeds in the earth speaking to each other, and wondering whether it is not time to burst open their narrow cells and push through

[7] St. Bartholomew, of which Dr. Greer was rector. He later became Protestant Episcopal bishop of New York.

the earth to where something in them tells them there is light and life. And one little seed more daring than the others comes up first and turns to a beautiful flower, and lifts its head to the sunshine and glory around. And then, remembering the little imprisoned seeds below, it calls back to them: 'Come up into the beautiful world; do as I have done, and break open your dark cells and, because I live, you shall live also.'" And I have thought of it over and over since, this positiveness of it. We must live, and what we learn on earth we shall practice in heaven. A seed does not come up a seed, but a full-blown flower; an acorn does not come up an acorn, but an oak tree. And so it is with us; what we begin on earth we can fulfill in heaven.

LATER. Courtlandt [Palmer] was here for two hours and a half this afternoon. He and his mother have just moved up. He must like me very much if he is willing to come back every summer, after absolute coldness and indifference on my part in the winter. I think I spoke to him twice last winter, and now the very first day after he is up here he comes and tells me everything about himself. And that "everything" is a good deal. He is working very hard and deserves an immense amount of credit for all he has done.

Sunday, June 18.

I am working hard at German this summer; I am bound to make some progress. So far there has been very little pleasure for me in reading it; I could not half understand things and did not appreciate it at all, but already after these two weeks I am beginning to. I wish there was someone to talk German to all the time; that is the only way one can learn a language. I have just finished a very interesting book by Werner. German novels have so much more to them than French ones; the characters are so much stronger. I wish I could meet some Germans, some German men. I would like to go abroad for all next winter and spend a month or two months in Dresden in a German family. Wouldn't it be perfect? Say, there would be a father, mother, daughter, and one very interesting son. Then

I would meet people and hear and talk only German. What a delightful castle in the air! Then after those two months, I would want to go to Florence and be in an Italian family, the same sort of a family, for two months and study Italian and art. I can't imagine anything more perfect.

And still, no, I would not do it next winter. I must stay in New York; I must see him[8] every little chance I have, and it is certain he is going to be in New York. I am sure it will be a horrible winter for me, always in a fear of excitement at a dance, always wondering if he will talk to me. And how often he will hurt me through and through! I believe the more he hurts me, the more I will love him.

I dreamed the other night that I was going to marry Lanfear Norrie. It was so strange. I was in my wedding dress and putting on my gloves, when suddenly I sat down and cried: "No, I can't, I can't, why didn't I break it off, like Amy?" Then I heard Mamma calling to me, and I got up to go. Then I woke, and a whole wave of happiness went over me when I knew that it had all been a dream.

It used to make me happy to have Worthy love me, and I once imagined it would be such a rest and peace to give myself up and just be loved. But it wouldn't.

Sunday, June 25.

Mr. Crosby came to see me on Monday. I was so surprised when I heard it. Unfortunately I was out at the time; had gone over to meet Pauline [Whitney] in Pittsfield. He was on his way to Williamstown with his mother and sister, but got out at Lenox and drove up to see me, letting his mother and sister go on to Pittsfield where they were to wait three hours for him. I am so angry that he should have come just the one day that I should have been out! But it is always like that. Mamma told him that I had driven over to Pittsfield, so he started hoping to meet me on the way, but as luck would have it, I had taken the back Pittsfield road, and we did not meet.

Pauline has been here a week, and I cannot bear to have her

[8] Gifford Pinchot.

go on Tuesday. We have done everything together and had
some such lovely rides, going out late, at half past six, and
coming home at eight and after. It is the most perfect part of
the day to ride. First you have the sunset and then, for a long
while after, the glorious colors in the sky gradually fading till
the stars come out and the new moon grows bright and silver-
like. I wish color could be expressed like music, that one could
write down and remember the wonderful blending and har-
mony of colors, the symphonies of light, the passion of loveli-
ness that seems to be everywhere in the sky. The wild, trium-
phant melodies and the soft, sad sorrows. But one cannot; one
can only feel them, not even tell them, but their memory
never quite goes away.

In the evening Pauline and I would sit until late by the wide
open window and talk, talk. There is nothing more perfect
than friendship; it simply gives the heart and soul a stir-up, as
Browning expresses it.

Sunday, July 2.

I cannot bear to think that the perfect month of June is over;
no other month in the year is like it, with its freshness, beauty,
and happiness. Some people think it a ridiculous waste of time
to go off alone by oneself into the fields or woods, and mere
nonsense to say there is a voice in every tree and flower and a
song in every brook. But it is so, and I am finding it out more
and more with a real, intense pleasure. Why does one live so
many years without finding it out? Perhaps so that we may
realize and appreciate it all the more when it does come. We
take things so much for granted at first; everything is only
made for our use or pleasure. But we find out afterward that
everything is made for each other. The flowers seem to be living lives and having loves as well as we ourselves. One can almost imagine their different characters, how some are proud
and unbending and others so gentle and submissive; how some
could be wooed and others not. And the trees! What secrets
they always seem to be whispering to each other, shaking
their heads so wisely. Are they the secrets which the birds

sing to them? It is only a short while since I used to think it
lazy, or a precious waste of time, to lay down my book or
work and let thoughts or dreams come to me. How foolish it
was! I believe that half of us do not think or dream enough.
There is so much to learn, so much which seems new about
us, that we forget what untold treasures we have in us.

Dr. McLane is staying with us now. I have a wild interest to
hear about surgical operations. There is nothing horrible to
me at all about it; it is simply a wondering interest that things
can be done which are done. For a long while I have wanted
to take a course in sick nursing, just so as to know some principal things; how to do up bandages and other little things. I
am going to ask the doctor about it. That would be something
more to do next winter. Pauline and I made a great many
plans together. Every Saturday evening I am going to keep
free; then we are going to the St. Bartholomew Mission or our
mission in Sixty-third Street. That will be some real work, if I
can talk to the men as I want to . . .

Tomorrow Beatrice arrives and Jay Burden, Alonzo Potter,
and George [Vanderbilt]. Harry couldn't come; he did not
feel like going anywhere, he wrote.

10

The Burdens

James Abercrombie Burden, Jr., who now appears regularly in the diary as Jay or J and who will ultimately marry its author, was almost too appropriate a beau. Adele used later to say that her parents' undisguised approval was a bit of a dampener in the early stages of their romance. He was handsome, clean-cut, athletic and rich, a Harvard man, the son of James and Mary Irvin Burden of Fifth Avenue and Newport, and a grandson of the late Henry Burden, the ironmaster of Troy.

Henry Burden had been almost an exact contemporary of Commodore Vanderbilt, with whom he was to share many descendants. He was born three years before the Commodore, in 1791 in Dunblane, Perthshire, Scotland, and died six years before him, in 1871.

As a boy, working for his father, a small yeoman farmer, he is supposed to have shown evidence of "marked inventive talent." He figured out a new method of threshing and mended the farm equipment of his family's neighbors. But he yearned to become an engineer and spent his evenings working with a local scholar and mathematician, William Hawley, until his family, convinced at last of his dedication and aptitude, sent him to Edinburgh for his chosen profession.

When he emigrated to America in 1819, he was armed with letters of introduction to the future United States senators

J, when a young boy, standing at left, with his brothers, Winnie (William) and Arthur, in front of Woodside, the Burden house in Troy.

Thomas Hart Benton and John C. Calhoun and to the great New York patroon Stephen Van Rensselaer. There is an improbable family legend that he never presented the letters, but waited until he had made his first million and then gave a dinner to which he invited these notables and, in Count of Monte Cristo fashion, presented them with the undelivered epistles. What is more certain is that three years after he went to work, in Albany, the stockholders of a little mill in neighboring Troy, known as the Troy Iron and Nail Factory, invited young Burden, who had been winning prizes at country fairs with his agricultural devices, to take over their management. This was the beginning of the Burden ironworks.

Burden's inventions formed the basis on which the vastly

J, at the far left, with three friends, in fancy dress.

J in matador costume.

expanded company rested. He developed a method of making wrought-iron spikes which was soon used in track laying on all American railways. He invented a machine that enabled its operator to make a horseshoe from an iron bar in four seconds. It was used by the Federal armies during the Civil War, and was so envied by the Confederates that Jeb Stuart instructed his raiders to be on the lookout for Burden horseshoes and pick them up wherever they could.

Henry Burden, eventually the sole stockholder of the company, was now the great man of Troy. His daughter, Mary, married Major General Irvin MacDowell, an early commander in the Union Army in the Civil War. After Henry Burden's death, dissension over control of the company broke out between his two older sons, and one of them retained Joseph H. Choate as counsel. The great lawyer came up from New York to reconnoiter the situation and wrote gloatingly to his wife, just before Christmas in 1889: "The Burdens are famous for protracted lawsuits. The father of these men had one about spikes that lasted for twenty years. And why should this one about horseshoes come to an untimely end?"

It didn't. The long and bitter litigation lasted until industry in the Troy area had begun to fall off. The city's position opposite the confluence of the Mohawk and Hudson rivers had become less of an asset as trains outstripped barges both in cost and efficiency. Then the automobile ruined the horseshoe business. Labor problems increased; business leadership declined. The Burden ironworks continued, but on a steadily declining scale, as late as the 1920s.

James A. Burden, Jr., a grandson of Henry's, even after his marriage to Adele Sloane in 1895 continued to occupy the family mansion and office in Troy several days a week, while his wife and children remained in New York City. The company was finally liquidated in 1940. Today, in Troy, only an abandoned office building remains, like the "vast and trunkless legs of stone" of Ozymandias' statue, as a witness to past splendor.

Yet the Burden family name today is not associated with

J, seated far left, with Harry Whitney, behind him, and Gertrude, at the Temple of Apollo in Corinth, Greece.

any such "change and decay." Marriage restored the capital lost in horseshoes. For not one but *two* granddaughters of William Henry Vanderbilt married grandsons of Henry Burden. Adele's cousin Florence Twombly became the wife of J's cousin William.

J, however, in the summer of 1893 was still by no means Adele's accepted suitor. He was to have some stiff competition from Frederick O. Beach, a handsome, dashing man-about-town, with a flowing black moustache, older than J by some dozen years and considerably more sophisticated. The only likeness that I have discovered of Beach shows him on top of a coach, in a gray top hat, reins in hand—the "whip"—on the road from Tuxedo to Nyack. It seems in character.

11

The Diary: July 9 to December 31, 1893

Elm Court, Lenox. Sunday, July 9.

I don't think I have ever spent a more perfect week than this last one; every minute of it has been absolute pleasure to me, and I can't think that it is almost over. I am sure it will have been the most perfect week of my summer. We have had beautiful weather, almost cold, with two hard thunderstorms, and we have been out morning, noon, and night. I must write what I have done every day.

Monday: Beatrice [Bend] and Alonzo [Potter] arrived early; I drove over to Pittsfield for them. That afternoon Alonzo and I went riding. Every day I think I like Alonzo better; he is so nice. Jay Burden and George [Vanderbilt] arrived in the evening. Always after dinner we would sit on the piazza talking and then, when it was later, half past ten or so, we went for a walk. Quite often we played "willing" games and mesmerism—made tables fly around the rooms, lifted ourselves up, and other extraordinary things. Jay has a wonderful power of willing a person to do a thing. He has a great deal of

The Garden, Elm Court, Lenox.

magnetism at all times and is fascinating in the true sense of the word, but when he really wills you to do a thing, it has the most peculiar effect on me, and over and over again, blindfolded, we did exactly what he wanted us to do.

Tuesday: We did a lot of things, riding, driving, and walking, etc., but Wednesday: Oh, what a perfect day Wednesday was! I shall never forget it. Beatrice, Jay, Alonzo, and I started on horseback at ten in the morning and rode over to Lebanon. Papa had sent a buckboard on ahead with our luncheon, so when we arrived at one of the first houses of this settlement, we dismounted, bought some maple sugar in the house and a pitcher of milk, then carried our luncheon up in the apple orchard and sat down under an apple tree and had a perfect picnic. I am sure that I have never enjoyed anything more. We were way off from anyone we knew, and we all felt wild. We stayed there about three hours, played games, climbed trees, and did various other things, and then rode home in the late afternoon. None of us have gotten over caring about that day yet.

Thursday afternoon was almost the loveliest of any. Jay and I went out at half past two and rode over to Stevens Glen. There we got the funny old farmer to put our horses in the barn, and after a good deal of talking, I persuaded him that we could find our way alone to the Glen, as he always persists in showing one down and explaining everything. I have never seen the Glen so beautiful; I have never seen any spot more beautiful than it was that afternoon when we got way down and climbed over the little bridge at the bottom of the ravine and sat down on a moss-covered rock in the middle of the stream. The rocks rise straight up some two or three hundred feet, leaving the watermark on their sides where the stream has gradually worn its way down. Huge rocks have fallen into the stream and are now covered with soft, bright-green moss where the water leaps over in little waterfalls or nestles round in sleeping pools. The afternoon was cloudless, and up through the opening of the rocks and through the trees we could see the blue sky, and the sunshine poured down leaving everywhere its lines of light and shade. We both said we never could forget how we felt when we first sat down on that rock and realized suddenly what the beauty of everything around us was. And then we talked, a lovely long talk of two hours. He has such interesting thoughts on different subjects, I enjoyed talking to him more almost than to any man I know. He gives himself up to you entirely, and the way he looks at you, straight in the eyes, makes you know that he is simply talking to *you* and not thinking of twenty other things. We were both wild on our ride home; it was all through the woods, and we felt like shrieking and screaming for the happiness of it all. I have not felt so absolutely well and brimming over with life since I was in Biltmore. Jay says he cannot imagine me sad or depressed; he had never seen such spirit in anyone. I suppose I will have a reaction next week. He is attractive in every way, and especially in his half indifference. He is extremely good-looking, very tall, very bright, and very interesting.

Yesterday I rode twenty-two miles with Jay, one of the

most beautiful rides up here. Up West Brook, where the valley is only wide enough for the road and the wild brook that goes racing down the mountain; across the top of Washington Mountain, which is like a high plateau with only low trees and shrubs and not the sign of a living abode for miles. It was on top of there that we saw the storm blowing up, the black clouds pushing each other forward, and heard the low rumbling of the thunder. We were at least twelve miles from home, and there was no place to put up for shelter. Then we realized what fun it would be to be caught in a thunderstorm way up there on that lovely grass-grown road, and every time we heard the peal of thunder it was more exciting. Finally in the narrow wood road, it was almost dark; then the flashes of lightning came, and then the torrents of rain. Jay made me put on his coat, although I protested as long as I could, and he rode in his thin shirt sleeves, and in five minutes was soaked through. From that time we rode home at a good fast canter, never pulling in the horses up hill or down.

We rode ten miles, Jay said, faster than he had ever been before; it is probably that which kept him from taking cold. I have never laughed more than on that ride, and every time I think of it I laugh again. The whole thing was such a ludicrously funny picture. Both of us galloping along in the drenching rain, laughing as if it was the greatest fun we had ever had in our lives; I with my hat tied on in front, for it fell off so often, and little streams of water and mud pouring down from it, wearing Jay's coat with the sleeves a great deal too long for me, and buttoned tight up to the throat. While Jay's white duck trousers and light-blue shirt looked appropriate for a hot day with the thermometer ninety! When we got on the main Pittsfield road, everyone turned around and stared at us, which only made us laugh all the more. I wish I could have that ride over again; I wish, I wish I could have the whole week over again.

Mamma asked Mr. [Worthington] Whitehouse up Friday night, but he could not come until late Saturday night. I have been on a long walk with him this afternoon. The conversation was as it always is, only about how he loved me. I was glad to see him again, but I would not want him to stay with us for very long. All my talks with Jay have been so intensely interesting that I could not help thinking this one today [to be] a contrast. And still Worthy is so perfect to me; how can I say the least little thing against him? He told me today that he would *make* me love him, that a love like his could not be all for nothing. But it would be an impossibility in every sense of the word to love him the way I would have to love a man before I married him. I would rather talk to Jay or Alonzo than Worthy, at least as far as interesting talks would go. Jay seems to be interested in everything. I showed him all the pictures in my art book this evening, and no one has ever enjoyed them so much.

Monday, July 10.

Everyone has gone, and I am quite alone, and feel lonely to a horrible degree. I think we have all enjoyed this house party, one just as much as the other, and now it is over, and it can never be quite the same again. I hate so to break up things! Grandma [Vanderbilt], Aunt Maggie Bromley, and George left at eleven this morning, taking Beatrice with them to Bar Harbor. I drove with Worthy early this morning, got home in time to see the others off, and then went out riding with Jay, our last ride, and we can't decide which was the loveliest.

Today we went through the Wolsey Woods, back on the Lebanon road, and tried two little wood roads to Ball Head Mountain. Finally we found a road that I was sure led to the top, and we began climbing, but when we got a good ways up the road suddenly it began to go down, so we tried one or two little paths, but they simply led to clearings in the woods. At last we turned around and came down. At the bottom of the road I saw a little boy and asked him where the road up Ball Head was; he pointed back where we had come from, and said: "Straight ahead there, across this mountain first, and then you will find Ball Head Mountain just ahead." We had gotten over the first mountain, I explained; why didn't we keep on? "Let's try it again!" Jay said; "You're not tired, and it's horrid to give up a thing." So back we turned and again

Adele's aunt Lila Vanderbilt Webb.

climbed the mountain. In fifteen minutes we were on the top of Ball Head, and then we were a great deal more than repaid for all our perseverance.

It has been the most beautiful day yet; at least it seemed so from the top of the mountain with the wonderful, marvelous view all around us. We dismounted, and Jay tied the horses to the flagstaff, and then we gave ourselves up to the intense enjoyment of it all. Jay goes perfectly wild over this country, so we keep each other company. After keeping quiet for a while, and then exclaiming a lot, we suddenly looked around and then there was a loud exclamation. My pony Phil had broken loose and was calmly trotting off in the field, while Jay's horse had gotten down and was beginning to roll, threatening every minute to pull down the flagpole and the pile of stones. I was thoroughly frightened for a few minutes. I thought first the horse would kick Jay, and then that the horse could seriously injure himself for he got his feet tangled in a most peculiar way between the stones and the sticks of the flagstaff. Phil was so interested watching him, that he let me catch him easily, and after a struggle Jay got his horse up. And then we laughed at the delightful experience and began walking down the mountain leading the horses. We both wished so that we had our luncheon with us, instead of having to come home, but we had to tear home for I had to say goodbye to Mr. Whitehouse who left on the early train.

Unfortunately we arrived home just too late. I am sorry, but I would not have missed the ride, or one of the experiences, for a great deal. Jay and I had a little luncheon together, and then not satisfied with all our exercise, went for a last walk. I believe perfectly that he felt terribly about leaving. He said he had never had such a perfect week anywhere, and he was so lovely, the way he said goodbye. I am going to ride with him in the winter often, and we are going to have a lot of reunions of this Lenox party. I only wish the reunions could come sooner.

Pine Tree Point,[1] Adirondack Mountains.
Tuesday, July 18.

It seems so natural to be up here, and I cannot realize that a whole year has gone by since I was last here. Emily and I came up on Friday. Uncle Seward [Webb] met us in Albany and took us in his car[2] up to Lake Lila. For nearly three hours I rode in the engine with him. It was so exciting. Uncle Seward ran it all the way himself, and I sat just behind him. He made a faster run than anyone has ever made on that twisty road before. Lake Lila is very pretty, and Uncle Seward's camp is the only one at the lake, so there is a delightful feeling of loneliness and being way off from everyone about it. We were the first people to sleep in the house. Uncle Seward has done all the furnishing of it himself, and it is so pretty and comfortable. Uncle Seward took me rowing on the lake in the evening and the next morning we took two mules and rode up

[1] The Webbs' camp in upstate New York.
[2] That is, his private railroad car.

to the top of a mountain from where the view was perfectly beautiful. We made all sorts of lovely plans for house parties there, but I am afraid they will not come true. It would be the most perfect place in the world to have some one you cared for to be with here, and the worst place for anyone who bored you. Uncle Seward liked Jay so much when he saw him in Lenox that he is going to ask him to Shelburne for the week after the horse show.

He is also going to ask Mr. Pinchot. Almost I hope he cannot come. It would be just like last year again, and that made me so unhappy. Sometimes I think I am changing my love for him; sometimes I am sure of it, and then again it all comes back again, and I think of him just as much as ever.

When Mr. Whitehouse was in Lenox he told me again and again how he loved me, and how he would make me love him. But there was not a single answering chord in my heart to all his passionate talk; even the excitement I used to have is gone. I want something new, something different. Is it my changeableness, or is it natural?

Elm Court, Lenox. Sunday, July 30.

I have been home just a week, and tomorrow I go away again, this time to be gone almost five weeks—first to Bar Harbor, then to Newport, then to Beverly. I am crazy to get to Bar Harbor again. I love the place and everything about it. I am going to be with the Shepards for the first time; before, I have always stayed with George. Of course it will be very quiet[3] and I will see no one, although Bar Harbor is very gay now. Mr. Whitehouse is going up on the first. I have not heard from him since he left here; I am afraid he was very angry at my going off with J so much, when he only had a day and a half here. I am sorry.

Last week I had a long letter from Creighton [Webb] and after the letter a long talk with Mamma. She had been wondering and thinking for a long time, she said, if Creighton could possibly be in love with me, and it made her terribly nervous to think that he ever could make me care for him, for

[3] The Shepards were still in mourning.

when an older man is very interesting and fascinating, he is very apt to make a young girl fall in love with him, and Creighton would be almost the last man in the world, Mamma said, she would want me to care for. I finally persuaded her that I never dreamed of falling in love with him, that the idea of marrying him had never entered my head, and that, besides, he had never once spoken to me of love and probably thought as little of it as I did, that we were simply very good friends. Then she told me how fearfully dissipated he was, what a reckless life he had led, and how terribly unhappy he would make any girl. I know it myself, and I am sure he will never marry.[4] I have never felt that Creighton loved me. Beatrice told me that he did, and from what he said to her, it certainly sounds as if he did, but I have never felt it when I was with him; that is, never very strongly. He certainly cannot dream of marrying me. Mamma is quite at rest about him now, but I am not; I wonder how it will be when he comes back here.

Loulie Baylies has been spending all this week here. If I believed everything she told me my head would be completely turned. As it is, I do not believe it, and a little praise does one good. I cannot possibly think that I am good-looking or beautiful or anything else; if I thought it, I would say so. There is no harm in saying you are beautiful if you are so, for you have had nothing whatever to do with it. But I have never thought so of myself; it would be quite a delightful sensation to feel it once, to feel that I was really beautiful. I have often stood before my glass and tried to be an outsider looking at myself. I have an easy natural figure, because I have never worn anything tight or never in the least squeezed myself. I have a moderately small foot, and I suppose a very well-shaped leg; only no one ever sees that. At present my hands are very brown with a marked rim where the white of the arm begins; that is because I never wear gloves. My face is also brown, and I rarely have any color. My eyes are black and my eyelashes long and my eyebrows thick. My hair is dark brown and brushed back off my forehead, with sometimes a little curl in the middle, and always done in a Psyche

[4] He never did.

knot in the back. I suppose I am moderately graceful, and perhaps very much so on horseback; at least, so people tell me.
But after this truthful picture I certainly cannot understand
how people can look at me and tell me that I am beautiful. I
do not believe it, but all the same, how can I help but like it?
That is only human nature.

Then people tell me that I am clever. Perhaps I am; sometimes I feel sure of it, and then again I am sure of the contrary
and I say to myself that if all girls had had the same education
that I have had, and traveled as much, they would be just the
same; only all girls would not have been so fond of study and
as crazy to know things as I always have been, even if they
had had the chance. Of course, that makes the difference.

The Shepards and ourselves have always been crazy about
reading, and just because we all have been, we have kept each
other going. Of the four of us,[5] I think Edith is the most
clever; she has not read more than I have, but if either of us
had ever done anything, she is the one who would have had
the most original mind and done the most. So far, I have
thought out a great many more things than Emily, and I
began thinking when I was much younger, which makes me
seem a great deal more than a year older than she is. I have no
better a mind or no better memory, but I have just as decided
ideas and opinions, though they may differ from hers. I think
Alice has read less than any of us, but she is very quick,
though she never takes for granted anything she hears, until
she herself knows about that thing. She is intensely musical,
though she does not play as well as Emily. Edith has the talent
for writing which she does not cultivate nearly enough.

I don't know what I have. I have always bemoaned my fate
in having no talent. I am sure that I could act, but that knowledge does me no good, because I never can prove it. The
French professor told me the other day that I recited marvelously well. I am taking elocution lessons from him, and he is
severe and exacting to a degree. At first I thought I could
never make any progress; he found fault with almost every
other word I pronounced, but during the week in the Adiron-

[5] Edith and Alice Shepard and Adele and her sister Emily.

Flower girl nieces at Lila Vanderbilt Webb's wedding in 1881. *Left to right*: Emily Sloane, Alice Shepard, Gertrude Vanderbilt, Adele.

dacks I made a new pronunciation entirely, and he told me the progress I had made was wonderful. I recited to him quite a long French piece the other day, and he made me very excited by his praise. He told me that I understood the piece perfectly, that I entered absolutely into the soul of it, so that he was able entirely to forget my own personality. He said I had an inborn gift, for a thing like that never could be drilled into one, and that with a good deal of patient study and practice, he was sure I would one day recite wonderfully. Of course I have a great many faults in the way of declaiming and intonation, but all that can be overcome. I have always recited a good deal for my own pleasure, and I know a great many pieces, but I have never made a serious study of it, as I want to do now.

But aside from comparisons and talents, I suppose I am what you call interesting. I have plenty to talk about, and other

Adele in 1879, at the age of six.

people's views on subjects interest me immensely, and I always try to get them. I can make myself attractive and I can flirt, which instead of being proud of, I ought to be ashamed of; only it is fun sometimes, in a quiet way. I cannot understand how some girls say they can make any man fall in love with them; I cannot possibly. I have never done anything to the men who love me to make them so; it has simply come naturally; nor have I ever said I will make so-and-so like me; in the first place, I couldn't, and in the second place, it would be too much trouble. I can understand men being interested in me, but I cannot understand them loving me, for there is very little that is lovable in my nature to an outsider, excepting, as Creighton says, I am very sympathetic; otherwise I am more or less cold and un-get-at-able, and no one knows, unless I want them to, what I think or what I feel. There is my opinion of myself. It is *true*, seeing that there is no object of my making it otherwise. I have often thought, if I could remake myself, how different that self could be from what it is now!

Bar Harbor. Sunday, August 6.

I am having such lovely long quiet days here; the weather is perfect, and I am out a great deal, although there is plenty of time for reading at home. I have just finished a book on the *Law of Psychic Phenomena* by [Thomson J.] Hudson, and it has opened up a whole realm of new thought and new possibilities to me, which I hope will not only remain possibilities but become one day facts. The experiments told about in the book are nothing short of wonderful, and even though there may be forty-nine cases out of fifty that prove failures, the one success shows that there is something to the theory, whether it be hypnotism, mesmerism, Christian Science, or anything else.

The only person I see anything of besides the Shepards is Beatrice, and she goes away tomorrow. I will miss her so much. I had a long letter from J last week; it was such a nice surprise, as he did not tell me that he would write. By some mysterious means the letter has disappeared, either blown away or stolen, and I am furious about it. Fortunately I had read it over twice, but there was an article on heredity in it that I wanted to study more, and I am so angry that it is lost.

Every morning we go down to George's and have a delightful swim in the pool. After riding, I enjoy swimming better than anything.

Mr. Whitehouse did not come up after all, I suppose it was on account of the terrible state of business affairs in New York. I have not heard from him once. I wonder if he will go to Newport.

Villalon, Newport. Sunday, August 20.

I have been here since Wednesday morning, but have not as yet done very much; for the two last days I have not felt at all well. However, I have not got the blues at all this year; on the contrary, I am in excellent spirits. It is great fun seeing everyone again and quite exciting. I have not been out at all since last February so it all seems quite new again. I don't see how people stand it all the year round; I should hate it above all things. The Van Rensselaers had a dinner the second night I was here. Worthy Whitehouse took me in. He was very unnatural and not at all as he generally is. I am afraid I made him very angry by going so little with him when he was in Lenox. Last night at Aunt Jessie's [Sloane] dinner, however, he never left me, before or after, and when Mr. [Frederick] Beach wanted to talk to me he stayed by the whole time. This afternoon he is coming up at four o'clock.

I have met a number of foreigners, none of them especially interesting, though one or two of them find me so. Baron Fallon told me the other night that I was the most clever girl he had ever spoken to, and a lot of other silly things. He was probably trying to make an impression, but did not succeed. The Englishman, Mr. Harrison, talked to me all the afternoon on the Gerrys' yacht and came up to see me the next day. He is coming here to supper tonight.

Richard Harding Davis is here, but I have not seen him yet. I wish I could for I would like to have a talk with him. I am not content yet; I want to meet still more people. Aunt Alva [Vanderbilt] gave me a big luncheon two days ago. I have never seen anything more beautiful. I sat between Mr. Whitehouse and Mr. Beach. Mr. Beach is lovely to me; I can't quite get used to it; he even asked me if he could come to see me when he gets back from Bar Harbor next week. I am glad he is coming to us in Lenox.

Aunt Jessie had a big dinner of twenty-four last night, and I enjoyed it very much, although I felt anything but well. Everyone is so nice to me. Mr. Gregory gives me a dinner next Thursday at his aunt's, Mrs. Baldwin. In fact I have something for every night this week and have had to regret several dinners I would like to have gone to.

Tomorrow I move to the [James A.] Burdens', and tomorrow night they have their dance. No one has asked me for the cotillion, and I am getting scared. I wish Reggie Ronalds had asked me for that instead of for supper.

I manage to accomplish some reading every day and keep my mind to it; otherwise I should soon get into a demoralized state of only thinking about society. It must be fearful to get so used to this life that you can't do without it. It is all very well to say that you do get some good out of everything; you do if you only take it in the right way, but I think you could only drain out a few drops of good from this sort of life and leave behind an immense deal of waste, neither good nor bad. For a little while, of course, it is not wrong, but for always, year in and year out? In the end what has one made of one's life?

In Bar Harbor Edith and I read aloud together such an interesting book, *Theosophy, or Psychological Religion*, by Max Müller, and so our talk was a great deal on religion; in fact, the general talk there was a great deal on religion. Here it seems to be left entirely out of this life. Sunday is the same as any other day, and no one dreams of bringing up the subject of religion.

I am thinking a great deal too much about people and about myself; it is not good for me. I wonder if I would get spoiled if I stayed here long. It seems so strange to have people admire me. I cannot get used to it, and it makes me so foolishly excited and glad. People have always been nice to me ever since I came out, but only the men who have cared for me have told me about myself, and now so many people do. Is it only a part of the Newport easygoing talk? Or do they think it? Why is it that it is a part of every woman's nature to crave admiration?

I have been going out the whole time these last few days; luncheons, dinners, tennis in the mornings and polo or golf in the afternoon. The dance here Monday night was one of the jolliest I have ever been to. We never got to bed until twenty-five minutes before six. The cotillion I danced with Mr. Harrison. They did not have it until after supper so there was a great deal of dancing before. I sat out on the piazza with Worthy. I suppose it was wicked, but the night was so perfectly glorious with a full moon. It is just exactly the same as ever with him. When he came up to see me Sunday afternoon he made me so excited that I was horribly tired and nervous afterward. I do not know how it will ever end.

I danced the cotillion with Mr. Harrison. Everybody I knew took me out, and I danced until I could not dance any longer. We had a second supper at five and then went out on

Adele on her honeymoon, in Japan, 1895.

the piazza and saw the sun rise. I undressed with my windows open and shades pulled up by broad daylight. It seemed so ridiculous to go to bed.

Last night Aunt Jessie had a big dinner for me. LeGlait took me in, and Worthy was on the other side. There was dancing afterward, but everyone was more or less sleepy so they did not keep it up late.

I am so angry; from my window I have just seen Mr. Davis drive up. He was at the dance the other night and talked to me for a little while and told me he would come to see me. Mrs. Burden came in and asked why I didn't go down, and I told her no one had said he was there. They were too stupid or too lazy to come upstairs, and now he has gone, and I am angry.

Tonight Marie Winthrop has a dinner out on Gooseberry Island. It will be such fun if it is only pleasant, but unfortunately it looks just as if it were going to rain.

Elm Court, Lenox. Sunday, September 3.

Such a long time since I have written, and there has been so much to write about. How can I ever get it all in? It seems almost funny to be home again and leading a quiet natural life after all the excitement I have had lately. I left Beverly on Friday. Mr. [William C.] Whitney brought me up to Boston and put me on the train for Pittsfield, after ascertaining that the train would go through all right. There had been a terrible wreck on the road the day before. A bridge had broken and five cars thrown into the river. Thirteen people were killed and thirty or forty injured. The only wonder to me, after seeing it, is that any escaped with their lives. The officials told us that a transfer would be made around the place and very little delay occasioned. So Mr. Whitney left me, and I prepared myself for rather an eventful journey.

I did not especially like the idea of being alone, for my maid, not speaking a word of English, is no help at all, so I was very glad when I saw Mr. and Mrs. John Kane coming up to me. They were also on their way to Pittsfield. A few minutes later I was surprised beyond measure to see Miss Houghteling with a friend and Mr. Pinchot get into the car and take a seat nearly opposite me. I thought she was in Biltmore and he in his country place or in his grave, for all I knew. It took quite a while to recover from my surprise.

I do not know if Mr. Pinchot's being with Miss Houghteling was accidental or not; I rather think not, for he seemed to do everything for her. She was very, very ill last spring and not expected to live, and is only slowly recovering; in fact, she was on her way to a sanatorium. I had always imagined that Mr. Pinchot was indifferent to little things, because he either did not notice them or did not think about them, but I see how wrongly you judge a person when you see only one side of their character, namely the indifferent side. He certainly was thoughtful of Miss Houghteling to a degree, from arranging her cushions and covers to rushing out at stations and getting her milk or bouillon, and when we arrived at the place of the wreck, he ransacked the farmhouses till he found a room where she could lie down on the bed, and was not content until he had seen her arranged himself and persuaded her to take a raw egg with whiskey. It was true gallant devotion and, as Mrs. Kane said, it would be in the natural course of events if he married her. He talked to me for a little while first, said he would come to us for the first Sunday in October, but it was a very doubtful promise, and I will be more surprised at seeing him here than I was on the train. He was not interested in what I said, and very soon got up and went over and read to Miss Houghteling for an hour.

We arrived at the place of the accident a little before six. Everyone got out, and there were a number of teams to take them around by the road, but there was so much confusion and such a crowd that Mr. and Mrs. Kane and I walked. It was a little over a mile, a pretty road through the woods with every now and then a view of the river. When we got up to the bridge we went right to the edge and looked down on the wreck. It was perfectly horrible. There were four cars in the river all on top of each other, a mass of broken timber and rubbish. There were men still working to find the bodies, though all had been removed but two. There was a feeling of sickening horror about the place. Everywhere were strewn mattresses and pillows and covers red with blood which told a ghastly tale of suffering. The wounded had only been removed a few hours before we arrived. The farmers and country people were still working with an almost tired-out excitement.

We went to one little house and managed to get some gingerbread and hard biscuits to eat. Then we sat on the doorstep and watched everyone. They were all on friendly terms, and people spoke to one another with a common interest in each other's welfare. I took a little fat boy on my lap and tried to amuse him while his mother took care of a crying baby. It got dark very early, and a drizzling rain set in. We piled into an overcrowded kitchen, but in a few minutes I found that I pre-

ferred the damp and the dark to the close stuffy room. I
walked around a little with Mr. Pinchot, trying to find some
nibbles for Miss Houghteling. She seemed to be his only
thought. I always liked her very much; she is so sweet. I
begged her to come home with me Friday night, but she was
afraid the long drive over would tire her just as much as going
on to Albany.

We never left the station at Chester until ten minutes after
ten, and it was midnight when I arrived home, whereas it
ought to have been seven o'clock. Now that it is all over, I am
glad I had the experience, for it *was* an experience, and one
which I shall not forget. Miss Andrews and her father were
on the wrecked train, but, thank heavens, in the rear car and
so were unhurt. I found all the family more or less worried
about me at home, but one forgets about that so soon. There
was a nice long letter from J waiting for me. He said he
would come up for over a Sunday when he got home, so we
will have some more rides. I also had a letter from Creighton.
There is a possibility of his coming home for a month this
fall. How I hope it will prove a reality.

My visit in Beverly was perfect, and I could not bear to
leave. Harry [Whitney] has never been so lovely to me in his
life, and I never dreamed he would be. I saw a great deal more
of him than of Pauline, for she was ill the second day and felt
too miserably to get up at all. I read aloud to her a good deal,
but it was always so beautiful out; one felt as if one must live
out of doors. I took long rides with Harry every day beginning with the afternoon I arrived and ending with an early
ride the morning I left. We had splendid talks together and
have agreed now to keep up the talks on paper. I was so surprised when Harry suggested it, for it did not seem at all like
him. We are going to read the same book and then discuss it
together by letter. It will be a splendid thing for me, for
Harry is very clever, and I will have to think a great deal before putting my opinions in black and white. I went out quite
often with his four-in-hand and got several points in driving.
Mr. Beach is going to teach me when he comes up here in two
weeks. I have practice reins with weight that I am using now,

Adele, in the left forefront, with three friends—Josephine Osborne, Alice Appleton, and Virginia Bacon—playing chess in Turkish garb.

on Mr. Beach's authority, so as to get used to handling four reins and to strengthen my arms. I am looking forward to it so much.

Mr. Beach was lovely to me in Newport. The day before I left he came to see me and stayed nearly two hours. I like him better all the time. One day we went on Harry's yacht the *Yampa* for luncheon and sailed around all the afternoon. It is such a delightful way of spending a lazy warm summer's afternoon, and I simply gave myself up to the enjoyment of it. Every evening I used to sit out with Harry until late; sometimes we went down on the beach and sometimes stayed up on the piazza. The harvest moon was just beginning to wane, but was beautiful beyond words on the sea, lighting up the little sails as they went to and fro, and making the yacht at anchor with its tall masts look weird and strange. And the beach stretched out in a long white line, and the breaking waves turned into foam silver in the moonlight, and the great rocks looked old and severe, and back of us the trees shook their leaves and whispered in the soft wind, and we enjoyed perfect summer nights together.

I do not know why Harry was so nice to me. I have always cared for him much more than he has dreamed of caring for me, but now it is almost equal. He told me about his ideas and ideals, how things were, and how he wanted them to be, about love and marriage and happiness, about work and ambition. We ought to know each other after those talks. I think Harry is absolutely true; if he keeps up to it, he will make a splendid man.

I was very sorry to leave Newport and give up all that life, more sorry than I ever thought I could be, for in New York I am only too happy to get away, and I do not especially care when I have to give up things. I never enjoyed going out as much as I did when I was in Newport. I was just in the mood for it and gave myself up to the pleasure of it, for I knew it would only be for a short while. There is a fascination in the excitement of it, and too much of it would be thoroughly bad. I saw Richard Harding Davis quite often during the last few days, and had some interesting talks with him. He said he thought Edith and myself and two or three other girls were types of the New American Girl, and he was very anxious to see what we would make of all our ideas and ideals. He told me he would come to Lenox for a day or two to see me, but I am afraid it was a vain promise.

I saw Mr. Whitehouse every day. He dined at the Burdens' the last evening I was there.

Wednesday, 7 P.M., *September 6.*

The sky is all red and purple and gold in the west, and deep, deep blue overhead, fathomless blue that you can look into for miles. The line of hills is black and distinct against the sunset, and one can even distinguish the separate trees growing on the top. The lake below is all silver, such cold shining silver. A little insect, and now a bird have passed my open window. How lazy and still and sweet it all is. A bright golden star has just come out, the only one in the blue heavens. What shall my evening's wish be? There, I will give it to the bird and to the soft laughing breeze to carry away for miles and miles and miles. Will it come true? Who knows? Who knows?

Tuesday evening, September 12.

There is a little new crescent moon out this evening; almost one cannot think it is the same as the large brilliant yellow harvest moon of last month which used to come up over the water in Newport, and then in Beverly, looking like a great red sun and then gradually grow paler and paler. This one looks so young and pale and white, almost as if it would die instead of growing larger. The fleecy clouds are still purple and pink in the west, but where the little moon is, they are soft and pearly gray and float along so lazily and dreamily, stopping to kiss the newborn moon as they glide softly over it. My evening wish star is shining brightly. Every evening it comes up at sunset time, and I wish by it, every evening the same wish.

Saturday, September 16.

After all the perfect weather we have been having it is too much of a shame to have it rainy and disagreeable now. All the week I have been saying I do not care what it does not if it is only pleasant when Mr. Beach is here, but it did just the opposite and began to rain as soon as he came. However, yesterday we managed to be out of doors most of the time. In the morning we went in the brake, and he taught me a lot of things in driving. I am crazy about it and go out every morning. Mr. Beach was very encouraging and told me he was sure I would drive perfectly. In the afternoon we went for a long ride in the pouring rain. I couldn't have enjoyed it more. I do not know how much I will end in liking Mr. Beach, if the liking keeps on increasing at the rate it is now. I should think if he wanted, he could have a tremendous influence over a person, and make them do anything he wanted them to. I wish he was not going away for all next winter. I want to see him more. I am thoroughly interested talking to him. What a contrast from how it used to be! Quite ludicrous!

LATER. It cleared off into an exquisite afternoon, cold and perfect. I went in the brake with Mr. Beach right after luncheon and drove for an hour, then came back and dressed for riding, and have only just gotten home. I have never had a more glorious ride. We went up on the top of the mountain, and the view—well, one can't explain impossible things. Also, I can't say how nice Mr. Beach is; it is absolute pleasure to be with him now. I did not know him before, and he did not know me, and the interest is not one-sided; that is the lovely part of it.

Wednesday, September 20.

I could not write yesterday on my twentieth birthday, but it will be a day I will not soon forget. I think if I took all the pain I have ever suffered in my life and crowded it all into four hours, it would just about equal what I suffered yesterday from twelve o'clock until four. It was exquisite intense pain that was impossible to bear. I do not know what got into me. The way he [Freddy Beach] calls me "dear child"; I can hear it over and over again. If I married him, would he make me happy? But no, I must not think of that; it is an absolute impossibility.

I had a long letter from Creighton yesterday telling me all about his journey across the steppes of Russia. He is not coming here on his vacation, so I do not know how long it will be before I see him. He wrote that he wished he were giving me lessons in four-in-hand driving instead of Mr. Beach who was rather a dangerous teacher.

New York. Wednesday, November 8.

I am horribly restless. I don't think and feel the same for five minutes at times. I have sudden waves of happiness go all through me, and the next second I am so blue I could cry. I feel in turn lonely, discontented, and then restful and satisfied. I don't know why it should be so. I want to be doing something all the time, but I don't settle down to any one thing. I have read today till my eyes ache and my head swims, and the book I read has made me more restless and longing than ever. *The Heavenly Twins*[6]—it is so tremendously clever.

How I wish I were in the country! A wild tear over the hills on my pony would soon take these moods out of me. I did ride yesterday, and it almost seemed like a breath of country air up on the riverside, just enough to make me crazy for more. I was tired today and did not go out. I wish I could have gone over to the Cathedral this afternoon; it would have done me good. I stopped in the other day late. It was almost dark inside, and one could hardly distinguish the few people moving around. Someone was playing on the organ, great full chords of music that made the stillness and the dimness vibrate with sound and light. I went and sat in one of the pews and listened and thought. It gives you a different feeling from what you have anywhere else. I don't care how wicked a person might be; I am sure an atmosphere like that would arouse all the latent good in them and make them long for something better, and it is just that longing which everyone needs. As soon as a person becomes satisfied, it shows they have lost their ideals and have ceased striving after something above and beyond them.

Tuesday, November 14.

This is the horse show week, and so one sees everyone every day, and after this there is the week at Shelburne. I can

[6] A novel by Sarah Grand (pseudonym of the English feminist Frances Elizabeth McFall), published in 1893, urging purity in men to match virtue in women.

scarcely wait for it to come. Mr. Beach said he would go, but he may change again. He walked home from the Mission School with me on Sunday and came in for a little while. I am afraid I have been doing all wrong in letting him see me. When I knew that this could come to nothing, I ought to have stopped it at once and not heard from him or seen him again. But it is so easy to say what one ought to have done and so hard at the time to know what to do. I am sick and disgusted and tired with myself. I wish I could stop thinking and arguing and trying to decide. Yesterday afternoon he gave me a letter he had written to me Sunday night. I cannot say how it made me feel. It is the first time he has said as much as this to me, and when he asked me last night if it had been wrong to write it, I said "yes," and then a terrible lump came in my throat and I could not say anything more.

He writes:

> Perhaps if I see you tomorrow and have an opportunity of giving you this, I may. I feel, however, as if perhaps it is wrong to write it and more so to let you have it. But why wrong, to tell you of my deep love for you which grows stronger every day till I do not know myself, and cannot understand my feelings? If you only knew the change you had wrought in me, and, my darling, if nothing ever comes of it, if I shall never be able to call you mine, your dear self has, unconscious to you, done more good than you ever imagined it had. Do you know today I told you I thought of so much to tell you, and when we meet it all goes out of my head? When I have your presence it is as if a breath of something so good and pure had passed over me that I feel as if I were really better than I can ever expect to be. I long to be good and to make something of life. You have stirred to the bottom a desire to be worthy of you. Oh, I love you so! As you say, it has only been a short time, and yet I love you better than anything in the world and would give up everything in it for you. If you only

knew how lonely and sad my life is! What does the world know of one's innermost thoughts? It is a double life half the world ever leads. Why am I writing all this to you, only to worry you? Forgive me, dear, I don't mean to; I only know you have grown into my life so, and intertwined yourself so around my heart, that I can think of nothing else. And that is why, if it is to go on like this, that it is better I never see you more, as it makes the pain only harder to bear. But if it is to be so, never regret, my darling, what you have done for me, for you have softened my heart, and may God bless you always for it! Good night, dear. May I tell you, perhaps for the last time, that I love you, oh, love you, dear, with all my heart, body, soul, and mind! And I pray so hard to know if it is right I should ask you to love me if you can. Will you answer this once for me, dear?

I have not written it all down. I cried after I read it, and then I got down on my knees and prayed to God about it. Are all the questions in life as hard to answer as this one? I feel so horribly selfish. If only I could tell him everything he wants me to tell him! But then the hurt in the end might be worse than it is now. After the first love of the senses was gone, would there be the love of the soul at the bottom? The love that rests in perfect sympathy and understanding? No, I am afraid not. He has had his life too long to enter into mine; for the time being he might, but it would not always be so. Oh, if I could only have done him the good without any of the wrong!

> *Shelburne Farms, Vermont.*
> *Thursday, November 23.*

I have just written to Mamma to tell her that I won't come home until next week. I was going down tomorrow, but I feel now that I cannot leave; it would be too unbearable to go back to the city just yet. I have had four perfect days here and now they are over. I feel as a balloon must that has been all full of air and floated way up in the sky, and then suddenly was broken and falls to the earth, a little nothing. I have been living simply on intense excitement, not realizing anything one way or the other. I have done everything with Mr. Beach from the evening on the train when we stood out on the platform and talked until one o'clock, till last night when he left. Up until the very last minute he begged me to tell him not to go, and even if I telegraphed this morning he would give up the whole trip and stay in town this winter and make me like him. "It would have to be one of us," I said. "If you did not go away, I would have to, because I must be away from you before I could know if I myself cared for you or if it were only you making me care for you."

I feel too horribly blue to write any of the things he said to me. I am tired and lonely today. It was a fearful strain on me yesterday, trying to keep up all the time. We took a long walk together in the morning and a three-hour ride in the afternoon. Then I sat next to him at dinner, and that was the hardest of all. It choked me to swallow, and about every five or ten minutes his eyes would all fill up with tears, and he couldn't look up because it seemed as if everyone at the table was looking at us. I thought the meal would never finish; then the frightful goodbye with everyone around, and I knew that he would break down unless I could be supernaturally cheerful. It is almost like a nightmare now. Everyone in this house party thinks we are in love with each other. I don't know what Mamma will say when she hears it, and I don't know what I am going to say to her. I wish the whole thing was over and done with or that it had never been. No, I don't either; I don't know what I wish, excepting that I might stop thinking.

Sunday, November 26.

I took the same walk today with Amy [Bend] that I took last Sunday with Mr. Beach. The view from the summer house on top of the hill was too beautiful; I have never seen a more glorious afternoon. If he only could have been with me! I miss him fearfully and think of him the whole time, but I do not

Adele's mother, Emily Vanderbilt Sloane (later White), painted by B. C. Porter, 1888.

know yet if I am very much in love with him, or if it is only still intense excitement. They have all been so lovely to me. Lila [Webb][7] told me today that if she were in my place and cared for this man, she would marry him. She said she was sure he would make me happy in a great many ways, and always be in love with me for he had seen enough of the other people to know when he really cared for me. Aunt Jessie [Sloane] has known him for years, and she said she never had seen him so

[7] Adele now calls Mrs. Webb simply "Lila," not "Aunt Lila."

desperately in love in her life. And I know he loves me, know it and feel it from the bottom of my heart. And he could make me love him. Only it was better that he went away and left me a while to myself.

New York. Tuesday, November 28.
We all came down last night. I could not bear to leave the country. I do not believe anyone loves the country and hates the city more than I do. I feel shut in and stifled here; I want to get away somewhere and scream.

I had the loveliest talk with Uncle Seward last night. He came into my stateroom just before I had gotten into bed. He said he knew that I liked Fred Beach very much, and he was sure that he was very much in love with me, and he didn't see why we shouldn't be happy together. He said such nice things about him, and I felt as if I couldn't thank him enough. I am crazy to have people talk about him and tell me things, but I cannot bring up the subject myself. Mr. Harriman said to me last night: "I would give a great deal to see you married to the man who has just gone away from here. He is ten times better than people think he is." I felt the color rush into my face and a fearfully glad look too.

But today, oh, how I dreaded to get home! I only had fifteen or twenty minutes with Mamma, for she was going to Madison to spend the day, and I tried to ward off the subject, but she asked me about it one of the first things, and I had to tell her. She only blames herself and never me, which makes it all the harder. She said we never could be happy together and that she never could reconcile herself to the thought of my marrying him. I begged her to try and forget all about it and never to allude to the subject. But I am afraid she will not forget and will only worry all winter. I can't bear to make her feel badly. I feel badly enough myself just at present, and horribly mixed up. I think of so many things that my whole mind is a jumble of a thousand and one ideas. I am going to be madly gay now and forget everything. But no, I dread it; I don't want to go out; I don't want to see a hundred people whom I don't care two straws for, for the sake of seeing pos-

sibly half a dozen whom I do. I want to do other things. I
want to be away.

Sunday, December 3.

Emily had her coming-out reception yesterday. I never had to
go through one of those ordeals, for I always positively refused to have a tea.[8] Of all the known society things they are
the stupidest. At least two hundred people told me yesterday
how sweet my sister looked and then asked if I did not feel
very old seeing her come out. There is only a year's difference
in our ages, but this is my third winter out, and oh, I am so
much older. And just now I am centuries old.

Possibly *he* [i.e., Gifford Pinchot] will come here tonight. I
am curious to know how it will be when I talk to him. I never
thought Mr. Whitehouse fascinating; I scarcely knew what
fascination was then. I do now, but one cannot live on that; it
would so soon go. Mr. Beach is the personification of the
word "fascination." It is no wonder he has made so many
women care for him. Is there a great deal of mutual sympathy
in our lives? I am intensely fond of outdoor life, of riding,
driving, and all exercise. But there are so many long, long
times when a woman cannot do any of these things, and then
what would we have to fall back on? Would he be interested
in the books I love so? Would my life with him keep on
growing better and larger? When sorrows and trouble came,
would he help me and give me the comfort I should long for?
It is all such an intensely serious matter; one cannot ask too
many questions and pray enough for the answers.

Sunday, Christmas Eve.

There has been so much to do lately that I have found no
time for writing. I am going to Biltmore next Thursday for
ten days. As usual I shall be delighted to get out of the city. I
was wild the other day when I got a breath of the country. I
rode way out to Riverdale and back with J Burden. It is about

[8] She did, however, have a coming-out ball, with her cousin Edith Shepard, in the picture gallery of her grandmother Mrs. William H. Vanderbilt's home at 640 Fifth Avenue.

Adele and J, on their engagement, 1894.

twenty-six miles, and we did it in a morning, stopping an hour at the Bends' old place in Riverdale. I enjoyed every minute of it. We are going to take another long ride on Tuesday. J amuses me. Every once in a while he suddenly begins by wanting me to do a hundred and one things with him. He came down on Thursday, and I have seen him two and three times each day. He walked over to the Mission School with me yesterday morning, sat with me half the time at the opera, and took me in to dinner at the Bonds. Today he went to Dr. Greer's [church] with me, came home to luncheon, and walked over to the Mission. Tomorrow he is again going to church with me and wants me to ride every day afterward. I am afraid he is a sad flirt.

I have seen a good deal of Dick Wilson lately but I am afraid I made him angry the other day for he looked daggers at me in church this morning. I had promised to walk back

A day's shoot in Scotland, 1902. Adele's father is cradling a gun in the rear, on the porch steps.

from Sixty-third Street with him this afternoon as I did last Sunday afternoon, but I did not think he cared one way or the other, and so I told Mr. Whitehouse I would go with him because I had been out when he called the other day.

Mr. Wilson has just been here; my supposition of his having been cross was evidently wrong. I think he likes me very much and, I am afraid, thinks I rather enjoy flirting. In fact, a good many people think that now, because my name happens to be associated with a man who is supposed to be the most dangerous flirt in New York.

I have never had such a good time out as during these last three weeks. I sometimes think it would be impossible to give up this excitement I am now living in and never have it again, and then sometimes I long to have it all over and settle down to a decided, planned-out life. Amy had a letter from Mr. Beach the other day, begging her to write him about everything that was going on. How I long for a letter myself! I think of him the whole time, and still I am glad he is not here. I would have been wild under his influence and unhappy every minute unless I could see him. And he in his clever way would have made me care more than I knew and have made me both happy and unhappy at intervals of five minutes.

I have seen Mr. Pinchot three times this last week. He came to call on Tuesday and dined here Thursday evening and sat next to me. I feel in a strange way as if I was looking at something dead. It was a part of myself, a whole part, and love has absolutely gone out of it. There was not one awakening spark any of the time I saw him, excepting the first momentary curiosity to know how it would be. I almost wondered why I did not feel excited when he said to me at dinner: "Please talk to me all the time now; I have not seen you for so long." The conversation dragged, and I was glad to talk with J on my other side.

If he[9] were to be down in Biltmore this year I probably would enjoy it again; never in the same way as before, but I would be interested and enjoy the talks; here in the city where he is never perfectly at his ease he almost tires me. And yet I do not wonder or think it strange that I loved him; I only wonder that I no longer do. Is it because I have had so much more in my life and feel how much more I can have? Some day he will make some woman very happy. Am I sorry not to be that woman? No, not just now, perhaps never.

Biltmore, Asheville, North Carolina.
Saturday, December 30.

It does not seem nearly as long as two years ago since we were last here, although so many things have happened in between, and of course this place is wonderfully changed. Still, it all seems so natural again. Edith and I have our same room together. Mr. and Mrs. Bacon are here, Pauline Whitney,

[9] Gifford Pinchot.

Alida Chanler, Clarence Barker, Mr. [Courtlandt] Palmer and Mr. [Benoni] Lockwood.

Uncle Seward has been too lovely to me this winter. He asked me to drop the "uncle" the other day, but I am afraid I will not get used to calling him just "Seward."

I saw Harry Whitney several times before I left. We took a long ride together Christmas day; then he dined with us Wednesday and went to the opera and talked to me the entire time, and the day I left he took me for a drive in the morning. It was on that drive he said some things which surprised me, for it did not sound like him. It made me feel in a strange way as if he were telling me that he liked me so much, and still I could not quite understand it. He asked me if I had meant by something I had said in Beverly that I did not want him to fall in love with me and that I did not want him to think I liked him too much, for I never would. The thought had never entered my head, and I do not see how he could so have misconstrued a very simple sentence. I remember telling him once that I thought girls were often unjustly blamed because they let a certain man go a great deal with them, and then, after all, it ended in nothing, and the world passes the verdict that she had led him on and flirted with him and then thrown him over, whereas in reality she never might know at first that he was going to care for her, and even after that, how can she tell that she never will like him? Time can be the only prover in all cases. There is so much injustice done because outsiders do not happen to know the truth about things. I told this to Harry because I thought he rather blamed me for letting Worthy go so much with me when he knew I did not mean to marry him. But he thought I wanted to warn him from caring for *me!*

He was fearfully embarrassed and unnatural when he said this, and at first I could not understand what he meant; it was so totally unlike him. But I know what it is now when I think of the whole tenor of the conversation that day—love and marriage—early friendship turning into love—an understanding between two people without the immediate result of anything—the difficulty of knowing just how much a girl did care for you if she had always been very nice to you, etc., etc. I cannot understand the mere possibility of Harry's ever falling in love with me, though I am sure now that I could make him—yes, perfectly sure. I do not think he would want to marry me for a great many years; he is only a year and a half older than I am, and is just beginning his life. I think he has always liked me more than any other girl, but I never thought he cared especially one way or the other until I was in Beverly, and then for the first time he seemed actually interested in everything I said. I always thought I liked him much better than he liked me; in fact, I am sure I did once, but I never dreamed of being in love with him and still less of marrying him. I think a girl when she is young wants above all things to feel that a man is old enough and strong enough to take care of her; there is a sense of physical protection in it. Of course, one feels that with an older man much more than with a younger one. I am sure that Harry will make a splendid man through and through—I have always said so—he has it in him.

Good heavens! How easy it would be to decide things, if the things were only to last for a short while. Supposing you could marry a man and live with him only for three years, and then be perfectly at liberty to leave him if you pleased and marry someone else? I know in that case just who I would say "yes" to now. And then, if I were tired and wanted to have a new interest in my life later on, I could go away. What a shockingly bad thing! I ought to be ashamed of myself! Uncle Seward made the very broad statement that he was sure I could marry anyone when I chose to. Of course, that is nonsensical, but there is a wild feeling in me that I can make people like me if I want to. It is wrong, more or less and is not going to do me the least bit of good, and just wastes my strength in a weak direction. With people whom I am really interested in, like Harry and J, it is all right, but it is silly with Dick Wilson or those men who simply want to carry on with me and be amused.

The only man I am in love with is Mr. Beach. There are probably ninety-eight reasons why I should not marry him, and two reasons why I should—the first that he is desperately in love with me, and the second that I care very much for him. I have not the slightest idea if it will ever come to anything. My family certainly do not want it. I think Mamma would like me to marry J Burden. As he is not in love with me, and I not the least in love with him, this is rather a useless wish.

I do not know what she would say about Harry. The thought is so perfectly new to me that I do not yet believe it, and I am sure half the time that I got mixed up in what he said.

If I married Harry, I dare say that through the years I would be much happier than if I married Mr. Beach. [Harry] would have interesting things in his life, possibly an interesting work, and we would be growing up and developing together. If I married Mr. Beach, I would probably live in interesting happiness at first, and after that—well, one can't help but look around and see the result of marriages where a man is almost twice as old as his wife. This sounds all so calm and scheming, a difference from the restless madness that is always in me!

I have just come in from a ride on that wild pony Punch that I used to have the last time I was down here. It was splendid; I feel so much better.

Sunday, December 31, 11:45 P.M.

The last few minutes of the old year! The others are all together downstairs waiting for it to die out, but I came up, for I wanted to be alone. I cannot bear to have it go. It has been such a full happy year for me, and I dread to think of what may come in the next. It all looks a blank ahead. I do not know what I shall decide, nor what may happen to me. Oh God. Help me in it; show me what is right and best for me.

12

Love and the
Unmarried Woman

The chaperonage of Adele's era, as we see it in the diary, is confusing. It seems to have been as strict in town as it was lax in the country. A young unmarried woman was not expected to go to a theater alone with a man unless they were engaged. Julia Hoyt Welldon, whose family were friends of Edith Wharton, told me that she had been less than pleased in Paris in the early 1900s, an era when girls were beginning to feel more liberated, to hear the sharp tones of the novelist, a few rows behind her at a play, calling out: "I didn't know Julia Hoyt was engaged!"

On the other hand, in the country, we have seen that Adele was allowed to ride for hours with J Burden in the Berkshire woods. They could even tether their steeds and sit alone in the wilderness, as long as they chose, without the wagging of a single tongue. Had nobody in the older generation read *Madame Bovary?* Perhaps an American faith in the wholesomeness of the out-of-doors, in the beneficent influence of nature, or simply in the cooling effect on lustful bodies of good, hard exercise made those Lenox rides seem innocent, whereas the tinsel-and-grease atmosphere of the theater may have seemed conducive to concupiscence.

Freddy Beach was deeply disapproved of by Adele's parents. Why? He was fifteen years older, but this, balanced by other virtues, might not have been an insuperable obstacle. What really bothered them were his morals. At one point it appears that he was living openly with a woman in Paris.

In Paris! But presumably half the young men in that metropolis, eagerly sought after by the mothers of virgins, were living, more or less openly, with women. Ah, but they were French. Young men in New York society may not have been expected to remain absolutely pure, but they were certainly expected to keep their depurification hidden from the public eye. It was not permissible for them to be seen driving in Central Park with a demimondaine, as they might have done in the Bois de Boulogne. And as the most they could expect from a debutante was a kiss, it was small wonder that they spent as much time as they did at stage doors or in brothels.

Did some of the girls in Adele's circle go further than kisses? Undoubtedly, but as they had to cover their tracks, it is difficult for us to know. I suspect that ninety percent of the Social Register brides were virgins on their wedding nights. I know from stories in my own family that it was not considered unusual (however embarrassing to the groom) for a bride over the age of twenty-one to be ignorant of the facts of life!

Adele shows how little difference there is in the soul between the generations when she expresses the wish that a girl could be with a man three years, and then another man three years, and then another . . .

Perhaps unbeknownst to Adele at this time, her cousin Gertrude Vanderbilt was also keeping a journal. Gertrude, indeed, kept more than a journal; she wrote letters to men that she never sent and invented their answers, and she recorded dialogues that may or may not have taken place. The border line between fact and fiction is difficult to define in the mass of paper in which she passionately recorded her tumultuous emotional life.

Gertrude, unlike Adele, whom she called her "playmate," was an artist who was ultimately to find an outlet in sculpting

Consuelo, Duchess of Marlborough, at Blenheim Palace, 1900.

and in collecting modern American art. But in 1894 she had no suspicion that any such future lay before her. She was intensely involved in trying to work out a relationship with a man, any man, that was independent of her being a Vanderbilt. In one of her imaginary letters she writes:

> I am an heiress—consequently I know perfectly well there are lots of men who would be attentive to me simply on account of that. When I first fully realized that to be the case I was terribly unhappy and wished I might be a poor girl so that people would only like me for myself. Now I have become used to the thought, and I face it boldly.

Adele, at least in her diary, never seems to have been bothered by this. It is possible that she did not think of herself

Adele and Gertrude Vanderbilt Whitney at Niagara Falls, 1897.

as an heiress. The rich always look to the very rich, and Gertrude stood out as "Miss Vanderbilt," the daughter of the head of the family, Cornelius II, who received eight times his sister Emily's share of the Vanderbilt fortune. Consuelo Balsan (formerly Marlborough), daughter of William K., the other older brother who also received eight times as much as his younger siblings, confirmed this to me when she emphasized that she and Gertrude had always stood out among the young cousins. "We were the 'heiresses,'" she said, and her tone made it clear that this was no easy thing to be.

Gertrude's frustration at being unable to be utterly candid with men was sharper than Adele's, but it was essentially the

same. When she enters in her journal the fantastical description with which she would like to have shocked the ears of a
stuffy Englishman of all the liberties allowed to American
girls at home, she was simply describing the world as she and
Adele would have gladly re-created it:

> I would stuff him about America. I would tell him all
> the liberties we girls have. I would say it was so long
> now that I had not had an evening stroll with a man,
> so long, oh how I missed it, and I would sigh and
> describe an imaginary stroll I had in New York. I
> would arrange it so that at this point he must offer to
> take me for a stroll. Ah me! I would carry out the
> farce as long as possible, we would plan where we
> were to meet, where we would go, we would talk
> over what people would say, and then when we got
> on dangerous ground, as we most likely would, I
> would burst out laughing and tell him I had been
> fibbing as hard as possible, and pick up the American
> girls out of the dust where I had thrown them. . . .
> Vain, vain dreams, never to be realized, even were I
> to have the chance my stupid self would interfere.
> Oh why have I any self except what I should have?
> But the dream haunts me, torments me, makes me
> long at least for the opportunity. To make a man feel
> for me, thrill for me, long for me, worship me, care
> for a little while once for me, this, in my present
> mood, seems happiness.

It gives one a sense of the forced innocence of the day that
all she yearned for was an evening stroll! Gertrude considered
herself very daring when she sneaked away from home in a
hansom cab to consult a fortune teller above a saloon on
Eighth Avenue. But even then she took her maid. The girls
were never without them. When Gertrude's family crossed
the Atlantic on the Cunarder *Lucania* in 1895, Cornelius Vanderbilt took his valet; his wife and two daughters were *each*
accompanied by a maid; and a special stewardess was assigned

to the party. Only young Reginald, aged fifteen, traveled without a personal attendant.

If men could not provide intimacy, short of marriage, at least women could. There was always the "crush." Esther Hunt, daughter of the Vanderbilts' architect, formed a violent attachment to Gertrude, and, as we shall see, to Adele. Gertrude returned Esther's affection. "I can count the thrills of my life," she writes in one diary entry, "they are so few and far between. Once it was when Sally (dear old Sally whom I don't care very much for now) took my hand. Again when Esther kissed me, and, I am ashamed now to confess it, when Mr. Crowninshield was talking to me that night at the Hunts'."

Gertrude did not feel anything wrong about Esther's kiss and probably was not even then aware that women could have physical love affairs. But her mother knew and discouraged the friendship. Esther, she said, had "no bringing up," and Gertrude assumed that this meant that the Hunts were not "swell enough." But this was obviously absurd. The Hunts were quite swell enough for anyone, and George Vanderbilt had Esther's father painted by John Singer Sargent and hung in Biltmore. What Alice Vanderbilt meant by "no bringing up" was that Esther was overdemonstrative and potentially homosexual.

Marriage brought greater liberty, but adultery was not accepted in New York as it was in Europe. Abroad, so long as the husband chose to look the other way, society took its cue from him. But New York added the qualification that the guilty couple must be discreet. The hostesses of house parties in Lenox and Newport did not, like Edwardian duchesses, assign adjoining bedrooms to a lady and gentleman known to be having an affair.

Some of Adele's cousins availed themselves of the latitude permitted discreet spouses. Gertrude and Harry Whitney both had affairs. Edith Shepard Fabbri was in love with Alesandro Fabbri, her divorced husband's brother, and ultimately had him buried in her lot in the Vanderbilt cemetery on Staten Island. The beautiful Consuelo, after leaving the

Blenheim Palace, Oxfordshire, seat of the Dukes of Marlborough, 1900.

Duke of Marlborough, established herself in Sunderland House in London, where one hopes that she had some consolation after years of neglect.

Adele herself had a house in Paris where she lived in winter while her husband was occupied with the Burden ironworks in Troy. She always liked a good time and was never one to spoil a party. No doubt she gave rise on occasion to gossip. Eleanor Roosevelt, on her honeymoon in 1905 with Franklin in Paris, had this sour comment to offer. Noting the presence at Voisin's of "*Mrs.* Jay Burden and *Mrs.* Harry Payne Whitney" with Bertie Goelet and Meredith Hare, she wrote home: "So you see, it's not fashionable to go out with your husband!" But one wonders if Franklin, even on his honeymoon, would not have been glad to join that livelier table.

Adele was always the one to hold the other men back, or try to. In Paris, or anywhere else, she could be satisfied with the appearance of admiration. Basically, she was as conservative as her parents and devoted to Jay, even when the Atlantic was between them. Some years after his death in 1932, when she started to go out with Richard Tobin, she kept another diary, since destroyed, which she allowed me to read. Although both

Consuelo, Duchess of Marlborough, 1904.

she and Dick were in their sixties at the time, it had all the charm and innocence of what she had written in the nineties. There was even a reference to Dick's "outrageous behavior" in a taxi coming home from the theater. But it was all right. They were almost engaged!

It is interesting that both Adele and her mother, after happy first marriages, should have found as great, and possibly greater, happiness in second unions, in each case to an American diplomat. In 1920 Emily Sloane, at sixty-eight, became the second wife of Henry White, a former ambassador to France and a member of President Wilson's Peace Commission, while in 1936 Adele, at sixty-three, wed Dick Tobin, a bachelor, president of Hibernia Bank in San Francisco and a former minister to the Netherlands.

13

The Diary:
January 1 to June 27,
1894

Biltmore, Asheville, North Carolina.
Monday, January 1, 1894.
Only a word to begin the New Year with. I made my good resolutions last night sitting over a little dying fire. The window was wide open, and the cold night air blew in. The stars were all out, and there was a hushed stillness everywhere as if something were expected. It has been so gloriously beautiful out today; it made me feel wild.

Wednesday, January 3.
Unfortunately I am missing all the glorious weather and wasting these perfect days in bed; it makes me too cross to speak. I had been looking forward to long rides every day, and I have only had one. We have the most perfect evenings here. Courtlandt Palmer plays for us for two or three hours the most divine music. He is a marvelous genius. I like Mr. [Benoni] Lockwood; he is interesting and clever. I love to meet new people this way who are totally different from society men. If

I marry a society man, it will narrow my life down to that set tremendously, and I will probably be very little thrown in with the sort of people whom I thoroughly enjoy talking to. I like discussions and good arguments. I like talking of books and a hundred other things, and I would miss it fearfully if I would not have it. But I will have it.

I had a lovely letter from Creighton [Webb] yesterday. I am sure Lila Webb wrote to him about Mr. [Freddy] Beach and myself from the way he speaks of him. Beatrice [Bend] told me that Lila said to her once that she knew a man who was very much in love with me and had confided it to her, but had never told me of it. It must have been Creighton. But I still never can really believe that he is in love with me.

New York. Sunday evening, January 14.

Now that I am home again I realize how much I loved it down in Biltmore and how fearfully I miss it. The last days were much the nicest. I got to know Mr. Lockwood very well, and I liked him much better than at first. He is clever, original, and interesting. We had some delightful long rides together and consequently some long, long talks. I have seen all my friends since I have been home, and now that I have seen them I am quite ready to go away again. Seward [Webb] is going to take me up to Na-Ha-Sa-Ne[1] the week after next for a few days. I can't get over his being so lovely to me. I danced the cotillion with him the other night at Mrs. [Ogden] Mills', and two nights ago he took me to the theater. I am afraid my head would be turned if I believed all the things he told me, but fortunately I don't. I had a long walk with J [Burden] this afternoon and another long walk Friday afternoon. I can't quite make him out, and that is just the reason he interests me so much. Mr. Whitehouse is so ridiculously jealous of anyone who speaks to me that he makes me often feel very uncomfortable. He doesn't seem to mind at all telling people how much he is in love with me. Of course, he gets himself terribly laughed at, and I decidedly object to having

[1] The Webbs' Adirondack camp.

my name thrown in with his. I am going to give him a good talking-to tomorrow when I see him. He has no right to interfere with anything I wish to do. Several things lately have made me more or less angry.

Adirondack Mountains. Wednesday, January 31.

The three days in Na-Ha-Sa-Ne were lovely. I was with J all the time, driving, walking, and talking together. The day before I left town I took a long ride with Harry [Whitney]. He asked me not to refer again to what he had said the last time. "When one wants fearfully to say something," he said, "it is invariably horribly difficult to say, and I am not going to blunder any more."

Everyone at Na-Ha-Sa-Ne thought that J was either flirting tremendously with me or else cared a great deal. How little outsiders can see into people's real feelings. I must confess that our relationship is a little difficult to understand, for no one would believe that at present we are living up to a delightful Platonic friendship. Of course, it will not last. These things never do, but while it does, I shall go on enjoying it to the full.

Mr. Lockwood has just been here for two hours. I have seen him several times since Biltmore. I like him. Lila[2] was very ill two weeks ago with pneumonia and gave us all a fearful scare. She is rapidly improving now. For two days I realized what it was to worry with every thought in my head and think the most unbearable things.

New York. Thursday evening, February 8.

What is the exact meaning of being true to oneself? How is one to know always what is true? Two things may often seem to be right, and how can one tell which is the most right? It is all so horribly difficult. One gets into the rut of conventionality and artificiality before one knows it, and then it is so hard to get out of them. One wants to do something different, and then the question comes up: is this only for a selfish

[2] Lila Sloane, Adele's youngest sister, named for their aunt Lila Webb.

desire, or is it because it is more true to my best self? And so often the answer does not seem to come. At present I am all at sea and so discouraged.

In his sermon yesterday, Dr. Greer said: "During this season of Lent let everyone bring their deepest and most heartfelt secret to Christ and let Him help them and show them what is the truest way to act." How I long to be helped! I don't see my way, and the light does not come. Some days I think it does, and the next day it has all gone again. But when it is there I feel as if I must give up this thing that is in my life now, that it would be better, nicer, truer. But I can't give it up; I am not strong enough, and I have not asked for the strength. I only ask that in the end it may come out best for him [i.e., Freddy Beach] and best for me. I have not once heard from him. Perhaps he has forgotten me. I sometimes wish he had, and then again the thought makes me wild. He could not forget after what has passed between us.

We expect to go abroad next month. "If we do go," Mamma said to me the other day, "I shall certainly not go to any place where you would meet Mr. Beach. If he is in Paris, we will not go to Paris." I felt so fearfully that I could not speak; I simply sat quite still and stared in front of me. I cannot keep myself from thinking of him all the time, and still with my free choice I would say: "No, I will not marry him, at least not yet. I want it to be just as it is now, but no more." It can't be this way, and that is what makes me feel so fearfully. It must be one thing or the other, and as I have not free choice to choose the one thing, I can't and won't be forced into choosing the other. Half the time I feel perfectly wretched about it and wish that the whole thing had never been.

I am going away again tomorrow. A party of us were going up to Shelburne, but the Webb children have severe colds so that Lila cannot leave them; Seward is going to take us to Na-Ha-Sa-Ne instead for a few days, and from there we will go to Shelburne. I don't see how he will ever get a big party into the house. Beatrice is going, Pauline [Whitney], Edith

[Shepard], Cora Randolph, Mr. and Mrs. Purdy, J, Dick Wilson, Jim Appleton, Mr. Munn, and a lot of other men. I am sure it won't be as much fun as the first time.

J was here last Sunday. We had such a nice afternoon. He came up to the sitting room, and he read to me and we talked for three hours. A lot of people say we are engaged. Grace Wilson[3] amused me the other day by asking me please to be nice to Dick on this party. "Even if J Burden is going," she said, "do be nice to Dick just the same; he is such a dear fellow, and you mustn't make him feel badly."

Sunday, February 25.

I am just back from Shelburne. The two weeks' visit was as usual perfectly delightful. J was with me all the time during the week he was there; he never did anything with anyone else. I blamed him fearfully for changing so from Beatrice to me. "You will never get a truer friend than she was to you," I told him, "and you have been a fool to treat her friendship so carelessly; you will be sorry for it one day, when you want it again and can't get it back." "How stupid," he answered. "When a person is once your friend, they are your friend for always, no matter what you do." "No," I said, "there is a degree of indifference and carelessness that in the end will become dangerous to any friendship. You can't trifle with that any more than you can trifle with love; otherwise you will wake up one fine morning and discover what you thought was a solid fact has entirely disappeared."

J is still in certain points an absolute blank to me. I can't understand his wanting to be with a person the whole time simply for interest's sake. A man may easily be very interested in a girl and want to see her often, but that is a different thing from the whole time. I should certainly think that J was in love with me, did I not know that a man's manner when he is in love is quite different from his. There is something in the physical contact with a man who is in love with you which is perfectly unmistakable. I do not say that J may not *be* falling in love with me. Sometimes I think he is. He came down here

---

[3] Dick Wilson's sister, later Mrs. Cornelius Vanderbilt III.

the day I arrived, and we went off that afternoon for a three hours' walk; then he came in here for an hour afterward. I am afraid I did a very unsocietyified thing. We took the elevated road up to 153rd Street, then got out and walked over to the river side and all the way home. It was about a five-mile walk, and as this afternoon was glorious and cold I felt just like it. He is coming down again next week.

He has never said a word to make me think he cares for me, but sometimes actions speak louder than words. Certainly if he begins acting this way with any young girl, I shall give him a good piece of my mind, for he will hurt someone before he stops. I am interested in him, thoroughly interested. I have enjoyed my talks with him more than with almost any man, but I have not the least bit of sentiment for him. I am positive that Mamma would like me to marry him; in fact, it is a thing everyone would say "lovely" to. But I know him pretty well. I know J would tire of a thing when it stopped interesting him or amusing him. He has already found out his power to attract people, and he certainly will wish to use it, either now or later. I said long ago that if he did not marry until he was as old as Mr. Beach, he would have had just as many things in his life. Of course, when you have once gotten used to a thing and hardened to it, it is more difficult to change than when you have only just begun, but in the one case the man has had it all and knows what it is, while the other may crave for it later. It is hard to say which is the best.

I had my first letter from Mr. Beach when I was in Shelburne, such a long lovely letter mostly about his trip.

"How much I have thought of it all since leaving," he writes, "but of that I shall not speak. I am so homesick, but I will keep my promise, only telling you that I feel just the same as I did the night I left Shelburne and looked you straight in the eyes and said goodbye. Don't forget me, please, and if it should happen what you said might happen, always be my friend, for I should give my life to help you, and I could not give up your friendship and our sweet long talks."

We sail three weeks from yesterday. The trip planned out is decidedly an ideal one. We have chartered the yacht *Rox-*

ana and are going to take a trip through the Mediterranean, stopping at Egypt, the Holy Land, Greece, and Constantinople. I shall be crazy if we meet the *Valiant*.[4] In a certain way I am afraid there will be some very bitter hours for me. If I told Mamma that I was desperately in love with Mr. Beach and would be utterly miserable if she did not let me see him, I am sure she would let me, for she has often told me that as far as it lay in her power she never would let me be unhappy. But I am very far from being desperately in love with him. I told him that often myself. Then I have been anything but utterly miserable this winter. I have enjoyed myself to the full, and of course Mamma has noticed this, and she does not want me to start over seeing him again and get myself all worked up. If I am in the same place with him and not allowed to see him, it will make me crazy. How I wish I could look a little ways ahead and see how things were going to be.

Sunday, March 4.

Mamma nearly took my breath away the other day by asking me if I would like to have J go abroad with us. She said she would ask him in a minute if I said "yes." George [Vanderbilt] and Clarence [Barker] and Dr. McLane are going, so that it would not look a bit funny to ask him. But *I* think it would. Mamma cannot understand that there is absolutely no sentiment between us. She told me that she would rather have me marry him than anyone she knew, and of course that is how it would look if he went with us, or people would say we were already engaged. In a certain way I would like it, and in others I would not. I don't care two straws what people say about me, but I do care what my best friends think, and I know what Beatrice would think of this, and I know what Mr. Beach would think, and so I don't want it. Besides, even if Mamma did ask him, I am absolutely sure he would not go. He also would care what people might say. Everyone in Cambridge is teasing him about me, and he is having a decidedly unpleasant time.

[4] The yacht of Adele's uncle William K. Vanderbilt, on which Beach had been invited.

He came down here Friday night. We were going to do lots of things together yesterday, take a walk in the morning and a long ride in the afternoon. The day was perfectly glorious, but unfortunately I did not feel very well so could not go out at all. I was horribly disappointed. He came in the afternoon at three o'clock and stayed until quarter before seven. I was on the sofa up here in the sitting room, and we had a delightfully informal time. He is coming again this afternoon.

He told me yesterday that he did not understand himself a bit, that he thought he must be fearfully undeveloped. I spoke again about Beatrice. "I can't pretend things," he said. "If I stop liking a person, why should I go on pretending that I do? It is certainly against your principle of being true to oneself." "Yes," I said, "but it is such an unfortunate way of getting into it. When you begin feeling that you don't care for a person, don't give in to that feeling; fight against it, and, after a while, it will come much less often. If you keep on this way you will bring a great deal of unhappiness into your life." "I have been told," he said, "that when I once care for a person with all my heart and soul, I will care always, but the feeling will be very slow in coming." If he went on the yacht with us it would probably be one of two things. He would get terribly tired of me or else fall in love. It could not stay this way for three months. And this is such a lovely way to have it stay; I would hate any change.

Friday, March 9.

I had such a lovely ride yesterday with Jim Appleton and such a nice talk. I asked him if what I had heard was true: that he had said that I had behaved in a decidedly queer way toward Beatrice in this affair with J. He had said, so I heard: "But isn't Miss Sloane a friend of Miss Bend's? But then, of course, women have not the same code of honor as men!" It made me feel fearfully, and I am glad I spoke to him of it. He explained exactly what his meaning had been; then we had a long discussion on friendship.

Tuesday, March 13.

J came down Friday evening, and we have been together morning and afternoon. He went back to Cambridge last night and would have stayed over this week, he said, if there had been a possible excuse to make. We rode to Riverdale Saturday afternoon and dismounted at the Bends' place and sat in the summer house for an hour. It was a glorious day, and I enjoyed it even more than the first time. Yesterday we took a long walk in the morning and in the afternoon rode up across Washington Bridge, struck off into a country road, found an old deserted place with a tumbled-down summer house, got off the horses, and sat down for an hour. It was delightfully amusing, and the whole thing struck me as being delightfully funny.

I do not thoroughly believe or trust in J. Up to a certain point I do, but beyond that, no. I am sure, however, that I could care for him enough to marry him. I think now of other things besides the love. There is a friendship between J and myself that I have enjoyed more than anything I have almost ever had. We have the same tastes, and we both have our whole life before us, and I am quite sure that he could help me and I could help him. Of course, this may never be. I scarcely know why I am writing it.

I heard from Harry Whitney the other day, such a lovely letter. It would be the same thing with him as it is with J. I wish more than ever that things could be decided for me. Everything is such a hopeless muddle.

We are off on Saturday. I am sorry but I suppose I will be glad next week at this time.

On board the Kaiser Wilhelm.
Good Friday, March 23.

This is our seventh day at sea. It is beginning, or rather has already begun to be, very monotonous. Fortunately, today we have a break. We pass quite near the Azores, and tomorrow we land at one of them, St. Michael, and walk around for two or three hours. It will be rather amusing. We do not expect to arrive at Gibraltar until Tuesday. We have had good weather

The S.S. *Lindula*, Indian Ocean, 1895, one of the vessels on which J and Adele sailed on their honeymoon.

all the way, only very rough, but fortunately I have been well all the time. The nights are too beautiful. There is a full moon, and I stand out on the bow every evening by myself, enjoying it all.

A week ago today I said goodbye to my friends. Such a lot of people came in that afternoon, but it is always more or less unsatisfactory. Jim Appleton bet me a pair of gloves to a box of cigars that I would be engaged a year from the fifteenth of this month. "Of course, I know who it will be," he added. I had another lovely ride with him that last week, and I also had a long seven-mile walk with Mr. Lockwood.

J came back from Cambridge on Wednesday. Thursday morning I had a note from him, saying that he had a case of German measles and was the most doleful person on earth, but that, come what might, he must see me before I sailed, unless of course I was afraid of him. As I was not afraid, and as he was almost well on Friday, we took a walk together in the morning, and another walk in the afternoon. I will not write

about it all. "I feel differently toward you," he said, "from
what I have ever felt toward anyone, and I feel very sure that
I will not change; otherwise I would not dream of saying this
to you. I am not going to tell you anything more until you
come home. Please try to believe in me." He has never asked
me whether I care for him; he simply begged me not to
change and be different from what I was now. Of course, he
knows I like him; I have gone enough with him for him to
discover that, but how does he know that I do not care for
someone else more? I told him I knew one man whom I
would have been willing to marry, but it did not seem to
make any impression on him. He sent me a little gold locket
the evening I left, and I have been wearing it all the time. I do
not know how it is all going to end. I am not in love with
him, but I feel that I could not get on without this friendship. I wonder so much whether I will see Mr. Beach on this
trip. I wrote to him two weeks ago, my first letter. It was
horribly hard to write, and I know it will make him very
angry, and then very sorry, and he will make me feel so badly
when I see him again that I almost dread it.

> *On board the* Roxana, *Gibraltar.*
> *Tuesday, March 27.*

We arrived here this morning at seven o'clock and came immediately on board the yacht. She is very large and way beyond our expectations. The others all went ashore this morning. I am going now in a few minutes, but I did not feel like it
this morning. A letter from Mr. Beach was waiting here for
me; it has been here for ten days, and in it he said he was
going back to New York very soon. I do not know whether
he has gone yet or not, but I sent my letter to him there. I feel
utterly wretched and sick and depressed. He wrote me that he
had heard of my supposed engagement to J Burden and had
believed it, and was on the point of sending me a cable with
his best wishes and congratulations. "I send them to you
now," he wrote, "in case there is anything to it, or for what
may be in the future." It was all different with him now, he
said, and he never would feel the same again. He had not

On board the *Roxana*, in the Mediterranean, 1894. *Front row, left to right*: Adele, Malcolm Sloane, Mrs. Sloane, Emily Sloane. *Back row*: Clarence Barker (at rear), the Captain, Mr. Sloane, George Vanderbilt, Lila Sloane.

known me before, but he felt that he knew me now, and I could add the words "and am frightfully disappointed in you." It is all my fault, this; it would be a relief if I could only blame somebody for making me so unhappy. But I have brought it on myself of my own free will. I have prayed to know what is right to do until I am tired praying. It is all a mixed-up puzzle, my life, and I am only happy when I give up trying to work it out.

LATER. 8:30 P.M. I cannot throw off this dull oppressed feeling which is all through me. Mamma asked me if I were ill, and Dr. McLane has asked the same question, several times. I feel ill and tired and lonely. I have tried to pray, but I can't. I wish I had said so much more in my letter to [Freddy Beach] than I did say, but I suppose it is better so. I wrote him that there had never been a word about love or marriage between J Burden and myself. "I may be queer and incomprehensible," I said, "but I am not heartless or changeable. I wish I could be different, but I can't." It will all be so different between us now. I cannot bear to think of it. I know just how wild I will be when he treats me in that cold polite manner he puts on to such perfection, when I have been used to something so different. But I am a brute of selfishness to talk this way! As if he could go on treating me as he used to, when I have done nothing for him.

Wednesday, March 28.

We are still anchored here in the bay. There is a terrible gale blowing outside, and it is impossible to get over to Tangier. It is rather a bad start to our yachting cruise, but we all make the best of it. I have seen the Rock of Gibraltar pretty thoroughly. Yesterday afternoon we drove all around it and walked through the fortifications. This afternoon George and I went around together. The town is very picturesque, and today we found the most beautiful gardens to go through, with the most luxurious growth of flowers everywhere. I went wild over a particular vine, purple-red in color and which grew in a profusive mass. Its name is bougainvillea. I have never seen it before. George got some cuttings to take back with him to Biltmore. I feel a little more cheerful today, but have still pretty dreary, mournful thoughts and rather a dead feeling all through me.

On the way from Philippeville, Algeria, to Goletta, Tunisia.
Thursday, April 5.

We are finally having perfect yachting weather, a smooth blue sea, and a clear blue sky. There has been so much wind and rain that we were beginning to get almost discouraged, but a day or two of sunshine makes me immediately forget the storms.

It doesn't seem possible that it is only a week since we left Gibraltar; we have done so much in that time. A week ago this morning we started but after four hours of horrible tossing and pitching we had to put back into the port at Gibraltar again, a leak in the boiler having been discovered. We started again that afternoon. The sea had gone down a little, but there was still a tremendous swell which lasted all the time till we reached Algiers Saturday morning at eight o'clock.

What a delightful day that first day was! It was disappointing not to get to Tangier, so we made up by doubly enjoying Algiers. It was the first part of African life I had seen, and it was all new and different and thoroughly interesting. The Arab port, with its little dark narrow streets and winding alleys and its queer people, was fascinating. One reads and hears about this life, but one can't imagine it unless one sees it. I looked into some of the houses; they open right into the street, the only light for the lower floor being the door, and that for the upper, a small barred window. I was not surprised afterward to see that all the life was in the streets. It seems impossible that anyone could live in such dirty holes.

The streets are crowded all the time. The people go around in an aimless, lazy sort of way, as if they had no object at all in life. The little children run after you and laugh and show their bright eyes and beg for a sou. The women pass you looking like white, silent ghosts with only their eyes visible. It is rather uncanny at first, but you soon remember having seen so many photographs of them that you get used to it and almost forget to think it strange. The modern part of Algiers is typically French, and the drives around the villas and back over the pass of La Femme Sauvage are beautiful, but I enjoy the old part of these towns much the most.

We left Algiers Sunday night and arrived in Bougie early Monday morning. A northeasterly storm with a drenching rain greeted us, and we went ashore under extreme difficulties, the landing being made almost impossible by the high winds. At Bougie we took three carriages and started on our long, two days' drive. The rain stopped at eleven, but it remained cloudy all day, with now and then a heavy downpour. We lunched at a little place called Lidi Rehan. Such a queer woman runs it. She calls herself a huntress, and dresses like a man and smokes, and rides straddle and has dogs and a monkey, and is altogether quite an original character, without being at all offensive.

We started again immediately after luncheon and then began the most beautiful part of the whole drive. It had been lovely in the morning, especially the last part, which reminded me of the Corniche. It was along the coast all the time, but in the afternoon we went inland right through the mountains. A little after four we reached the Gorge of Chabet. I have been over nine of the most famous passes in Europe but I have never seen anything as beautiful as this gorge. It is simply indescribable. It made me feel solemn and quiet, and then oppressed and horribly small and insignificant. And now that I look back on it, it all seems wonderfully grand and marvelously beautiful. The rocks rise on either side of you six thousand feet, with only about a hundred feet in between. Through this rushes the river, and out of the mass of solid rock this road is built. The French did this wonderful piece of engineering some ten or fifteen years ago.

We came out of the gorge just as it was beginning to grow dark and in a few minutes more had stopped at the inn where we were to spend the night. Such a primitive place I have certainly never been in. Charata is its name. There were a few Arabs sleeping or eating and drinking in the main hall. We were supposed to take our dinner here, but by a few bribes we secured a room opening on to this, and there managed to eat rather a measly dinner. It struck me as being so funny on my way to bed, to stop at the hall table, take a candle, light it by the one gas lamp, then climb up the narrow stairs and through the dark hall to this little bedroom Emily and I had together. Fortunately the room looked clean, and we passed a comfortable night.

Palermo, Sicily. Sunday, April 8.

It is too beautiful out at this very minute. We are in the bay of Palermo. It is evening. There is a new moon out for the first time, and the stars look less bright in consequence; little sailboats and rowboats are gliding up and down. Someone is singing in the distance, and someone else is playing. The mountains rise up cold and dark from the sea, with a look of bold decision about them. I feel like dreaming. That is just what I have been doing, thinking and dreaming and idealizing, sitting on the upper deck, wrapped in a shawl with the whole harbor stretched out before me.

We had our first mail yesterday. There were two letters for me from J. The first one nineteen pages long, the second, seven. He had written me every day but one since I left. Such long interesting letters. He told me again that he liked me better than anyone he had ever known. "I have cared for two people," he wrote, "but it was a very superficial sort of caring that I soon got over, but I will not get over this; I feel very sure of it." He told me that he believed and trusted in me absolutely. I am so glad; I hope I never will do anything to break that trust. Then he told me over and over again how he missed me. The letters made me very, very glad. I also heard from Creighton and Seward and Beatrice and Edith. What a pleasure letters are when one is so far from home!

We spent two days at Tunis. In a certain way it is much more interesting than Algiers. The Arab quarter is much more extensive. Half of the streets are built under the ground, but strange to say they are perfectly ventilated and not in the least degree close or disagreeable. The effect, however, is very peculiar. You see through the opening, grass and flowers and trees growing overhead. I spent most of my time in this quarter, though we drove out to see one or two palaces, and then of course went to the ruins of Carthage, or rather the little which remains of the ruins. From there we came up here to Sicily. The coast scenery is too beautiful and doing it the way we are in a yacht is really the only way to enjoy it. I fully expect by the end of the next few days to be entirely intoxicated with the beauty of all this. We leave tomorrow morning for Messina.

Cairo. Sunday, April 15.

Scene: On the balcony of Shepheard's Hotel, Cairo. Sunday afternoon. A blue cloudy sky and a wind blowing from the desert occasioning blinding waves of dust. Constantly changing and absorbingly interesting scenes in the street below. Does one ever get tired of watching these scenes? To me they are all new and strange. We have been in Cairo only three hours. Almost I cannot realize that we are actually here. I have read and heard and thought so much of Cairo as a thing of the dim future that I cannot make up my mind that it has become now the present, and that I am really in Egypt.

We arrived in Alexandria last night after a rough trip of three days from Malta, and we left there early this morning and came on here.

I was sorry to leave Sicily, terribly sorry; we had one day after another of perfect scenery there, and it reached its culmination at Taormina, where we went on Tuesday from Messina. I have only seen one place in the world as beautiful as Taormina; that place is Orizaba in Mexico. Such places as these live forever in one's memory, but they are utterly impossible to describe. I was up at six o'clock [the] morning when we left Messina, so as to be able to watch the scenery on the coast all the way down to Taormina. The misty morning light, the dim outline of Italy on the other side, the castles and villages on the rough great rocks of Sicily, the snow-covered mountain of Etna rising out of the sea and going up, up into the skies, the blue sea and the blue heaven; all this was a happiness to me then, and will be a happiness to me always.

We spent an afternoon in Syracuse visiting the Roman and Greek amphitheaters and the Cave of Dionysius, and the old church where Saint Paul is supposed to have preached during the three days he spent in Syracuse. From there we went on to Malta. I have had another letter from J, another letter which made me as glad as the first ones.

Wednesday evening, April 18.

I am writing my journal at present simply from a sense of duty. I do not feel in the least bit like it. I do so much and see so much during the day that when the night comes I am too tired to think. This morning we hired a steam launch and went up the Nile as far as Memphis. It took two hours. I am glad to have had this little glimpse of life on the Nile. I can easily imagine the fascination of it, that is, about three weeks of it. Three months, the usual time to get up to the Third Cataract and back, would be a little too long. We had donkeys meet us at the landing. It is a five-mile ride to the Pyramids, and a great part of it in the desert. I don't feel like describing anything, so I am not going to. I have written my longest letters to J, and when one has once described a thing, one cannot describe it again, unless the spirit moves me, and unfortunately it is not moving me. I have had two letters from J since I have been here. He has written me by every steamer. We leave here tomorrow and go up to Alexandria and from there we go to Palestine. How new and interesting and delightful it all is!

Hôtel Liverpool, Paris. Friday, May 4.

Paris has never seemed less beautiful and less lovely than it does to me this year. There is a cold, cruel wickedness in it all. I feel chilled and depressed. The first news I heard when I arrived here two days ago was that Mr. Beach was in Paris. I never dreamed he was here. He wrote me he was going home the first of April. Would to God that he had! They have told me things about him which made me cry myself to sleep the first night, and have made my heart and head ache since. He is leading openly a bad life here in Paris. That means so much. It is only these last two years that I have realized what one side of life looked like, such a horrible, fascinating side of life.

I remember so well Mr. Beach telling me once that if he lost me, all the good would go out of his life, and he would not care what became of him. I told him how cowardly I thought that was, and how miserably weak. But it is just what he has done. A great many of his friends refuse to have anything to do with him. I am sick at the thought of it all. The Fred Vanderbilts dined here last night. After dinner Aunt Lulu came over and sat down on the sofa by me. "Adele," she said, "I

wish I could do something for Fred Beach before he goes utterly to the bad. I know that you have had influence on him;
try and do something for him now." But what can I do?
Mamma won't let me see him, and he has not tried to see me. I
can't write; what would I say? I can pray to God, and I have
from my very soul.

The thought of writing took hold of me, and on the spur of
the minute, without any reflection, I wrote, and I have sent
the letter before I can be sorry for it. It may be reckless and
mad of me, but I could not help it; something seemed to make
me write. He will be horribly angry and hate me for writing
on such a subject; what man wouldn't? I had no business to
interfere. I am fearfully excited and shivering all over.

Ah! The music was a relief. I can't play much, but I would
not give up the little for a great deal; it is such a comfort.
And now I shall go to bed. I sleep so little. I think of nothing
else but these horrid weighing-down thoughts. Writing is
generally a relief, but it isn't now. I have not felt like opening
my journal.

Saturday evening, May 5.

He answered my letter and he was not angry. After I read
[his reply] I sat quite still for a long, long while; how long I
did not know until Emily came in and asked me what I had
been doing for the last two hours. All day I have been nervous
and excited. The family lunched out at one of the cafés, and I
stayed home alone, on pretense of being very tired. I have
tried to read but I can't put my mind to it. I am so glad I
wrote that letter, so very glad. This is his answer:

> No, no, no, I am not so utterly indifferent to myself
> as you say I am, if my feelings are at all evidence to
> what I felt on receiving your letter this morning.
> God knows I never meant to give you any pain, and
> I shall never forgive myself for having done so. I did
> not think you cared enough for even that. I cannot
> tell you what overcame me after reading your kind

words. Make me angry, no, never, but oh, so miserable and unhappy, and I am ill too. I don't know what
is the matter with me. Please, please don't write to
me again; I shall never see you more. Forget me, for
I am not worth a thought. I don't know what they
have told you about me. Anything might be true
since I arrived at Nice, but if they said anything of
me before that, it is as false as anything false ever
was. Yes, you were and always shall be an influence
on my life for good. I gave you all the good there
was in me. But now I feel I have grown hard and
indifferent. But times come over me when I think of
your sweet face and the good we talked about, and
then I am wretched. But I must not write like this to
you. I am utterly alone in the world and have only
my friends to rely on, but when they turn out as
some I have had, there is little faith to be put in
them, so it is better I should be as I am. I have been
through a great deal in the last five months, and my
faith in mankind has been terribly shaken. But you
are young; you have the whole world before you;
make the most of it; don't let my gloomy thoughts
affect you; for you there is a great deal. My life is
more than half spent. Oh, if I could only go to some
quiet spot and live out as a man the rest of it! I shall
always think of you as the one good and best that
ever influenced it. Your letter from Gibraltar I never
received. I promise on my return to send it to you
unopened. I never heard if you got mine which I
sent. Oh, please let me feel you have forgiven me and
that I will never make you unhappy! I shall try to be
better, if only for your sake. Goodbye, and may
God bless you, for all your kindness to me.

I would give anything in the world if I could help him,
anything. I want to see him; I want to talk to him, but I can't.
I can't write now. I wish everyone knew the lovely side of his
character which I know.

Thursday, May 10.

I have never spent such long horrible days in my life. Indoors
I am crazy to be out for the mere possibility of meeting him;
outdoors I am restless, and my eyes ache with straining, and I
long to get back. Is it always going to be this way? I never
dreamed that I was so much under his influence. I wish, oh, I
wish a thousand, thousand things!

I saw him for the first time two days ago. He was walking
with Mr. [Howard] Cushing and another man, and I was driving with Papa. I don't think I bowed; I have a vague recollection
of only looking and then of feeling horribly cold; then Papa
said something, and two minutes later we were at the hotel. I
was trembling all over and felt sick and dizzy. It was the first
time I had seen him since the night he left Shelburne. That
day with all its recollections and the evening with its goodbye. How often I have wondered and thought how it would
be when I saw him again. I have an intense, longing desire to
see him and talk to him. I hate Aunt Alva for saying the
things she does say of him; more than half of them are untrue.
I am selfishly morbid and unhappy, but I cannot throw it off.

Sunday, May 13.

Emily and I went this morning to St-Sulpice: Carolus-Duran[5]
gave us a letter to the organist, Mr. [Charles Marie] Widor,
one of the best composers and musicians in France. He asked
us to come up to the organ loft with him, and we sat down by
him and had one of the most perfect Sunday mornings I have
ever had. He played the Saint-Saëns Mass and then one of his
nine symphonies. It was gloriously beautiful. The organ is the
largest in Paris, with five keyboards, and in the chancel there
was a choir of two hundred men. The music is still throbbing
in my head and vibrating all through me—the long swelling
chords, the low deep tones, the blending voices, the chanting
priests, the incense, the light, the holiness of it all! The Catholic service without music is nothing; with music it is everything. I shall remember this morning always. Above all things,

---

[5] The professional name of Charles Auguste Émile Durand, a French
portrait painter; teacher of John Singer Sargent.

I was longing most for music now; I needed it and it has helped me.

Creighton Webb arrives here tonight. I have had three letters from him since I have been in Paris. I wonder if he really is only coming on to see me. He wrote that he would have to return to St. Petersburg, as all his affairs were not quite finished. He resigned his position a month ago. I am crazy to see him, crazy to talk to him about a hundred things. I wonder if he will be disappointed in me and think me changed. He must believe in me and trust me; I couldn't stand being hurt any more.

Uncle Willie [Vanderbilt] leaves tomorrow to join his yacht at Marseilles. Mr. Beach and Louis Webb go with him. I am glad in a fearfully disappointed sorry kind of way. Perhaps the restless, excited feeling will go now. I often think and wonder how it is all going to be when I get home and see J again. I still hear from him by almost every mail. I never would promise him anything until I felt quite differently from what I do now. If he asks me about myself I shall tell him everything I have written here. I do not know myself; I am not sure of myself; it is horrible but it is true, and until I do I shall never bind myself to any promise—with the hope that it will all come right some day. It would be wrong to the man; it would be just as wrong to me.

Wednesday, May 16.

Creighton did not arrive until this morning. He came here to luncheon. I was more glad even than I thought I would be to see him, but we did not have very much time for a talk, and I am afraid it will be like this all the time; there are nothing but interruptions here. He told me a lot about himself and asked me a lot about myself. He told me that he loved me more than anyone in the world, but that he never intended making love to me and that I must not be in the least bit afraid of him. "It would be quite a different thing," he added, "if you were ten years older or I ten years younger. I would try then. But now at least we can always be friends." Then he asked me about Mr. Beach and about J Burden. Then he told me more of his plans, and how he had only come on here to see me, and he was sorry and cross because I could not go out with him here or visit the Salon or Champs de Mars. He was just the same as he has always been. I am looking forward to tomorrow.

It has been such fun lately taking driving lessons on the road from Mr. Hocolett. I went out with him for the third time today, and drove for an hour and twenty minutes without once giving up the reins. He made me go through the little narrow streets of Passy which look like an impossibility. One has to be very quick and on the *qui vive* every second. He gave me a good deal of encouragement today, and I feel myself that I have improved. I only wish I had time for more lessons.

Saturday, May 19.

I have seen Creighton every day. He told Papa that he cared for me more than he could tell, but he did not want either Mamma or him to worry about me as he never intended to broach the subject to me. But he has broached it, only in such a way as not to make me feel badly. He told me that he loved me a great deal more than Mr. Beach had ever dreamed of loving me, and he told me that nothing he had ever done had been half so hard as last year when he went away and gave up absolutely all hope of ever trying to make me love him. He told Lila Webb about it when she asked him what had persuaded him to take the position in St. Petersburg.

He dined with us last night and went afterward to the Opéra-Comique. Coming home I went in a cab with him, and he told me about some trouble he had gotten into lately and asked my advice. "I tell you things," he said, "I never would tell anyone else. I don't know why, but I feel that you can help me; I feel like being a different man when I see you." He was over at the Champs de Mars this afternoon and we walked around together for an hour. He also went to Carolus-Duran's studio this morning, and we had a little talk there. Tomorrow will be the last day I shall see him. We go to London early Monday morning. He wants to go on too, but there is a limit to my parents' indulgence, and no matter what Creighton might say, they would soon worry if this sort of thing kept up for long. He told me how lonely he had been in St. Petersburg and how he would not go back there again unless he married, and then how he could not marry anyone in justice to them with the thought of another girl always in between. "Yes," he said, "I don't believe you have any idea how much I think of you and how much you are in my life. I wish it had never been so, but now that it is I have to make the best of it."

I can't get over the wonder of it. It seems so utterly impossible that he should like me; it doesn't somehow seem at all real, but more as if I were an outsider looking in, for the whole thing doesn't seem quite to touch me personally. I can't explain, but it is a queer feeling.

Hotel Bristol, London. Sunday, May 27.

I heard this morning such an interesting sermon by Mr. [H. R.] Haweis on the definite indefiniteness of God. There were a lot of thoughts to carry away with one, and I hope I won't lose them.

There are only three more days before we sail. In certain ways I do not want to go at all; in fact, I almost dread it, and I think and wonder and plan until I am utterly tired. I would like to have the next six months in my life as an absolute blank, nothing to decide, nothing definite, no new excitements, just the pleasure of living and enjoying life for itself alone. I would forget many things that I am now beginning to forget slowly, and then I would begin all over again the life which looks to me so bright and happy in my dreams.

I wonder how Beatrice would feel if I married J. She has been so perfect about it all winter; I mean about his caring more for me than he did for her. It made me often feel like a mean beast, and I hated myself, though I could not quite see where the blame began and where it stopped. I was interested in J when I first began to know him last July, but I do not think I ever tried to make him like me, and a thousand times less to take him away from Beatrice. Her friendship is more to me than anything I have; I could not give it up, and God knows that I have never willingly hurt her.

I had often wondered what it would be in a friendship when the same man cared for both girls, and when one cared for him but he ended by caring more for the other. That is what it has been in our case, but there has been absolute trust and frankness between us, and the friendship has grown stronger instead of less. But that is due to Beatrice's unselfishness. I wonder if I could have been the same. I wonder if J turned now and liked Beatrice again if I would be jealous. No, I would have such a contempt for him that I could not even be jealous, because a thing like that could not happen twice, but if he should care for any other girl, ah, that would be quite a different thing! Yes, I should be jealous then; I want him to care for me; sometimes I think I don't realize how much I want it, because I feel sure of it, much surer than I did before coming abroad.

Supposing I should be mistaken? I shall know very soon. I have asked him to spend three weeks from today with us at Lenox, and I shall probably see him the day we arrive in New York. I had a letter from him yesterday, saying he should come to town that day. There has never been a word of love between us, but our conversations could not go on in the same strain they did before I sailed. Common sense tells me that. Then how will it be? That is what I have asked myself a thousand times.

Elm Court, Lenox. Sunday, June 10.

We came up here the day after we arrived and oh, how glad I was to be in the country again and how beautiful everything looks! Of course, I have ridden to my heart's content, and rushed around the place generally. We had a splendid trip across on the *Majestic*, not one rough day, and we arrived in New York Wednesday at half past ten. Almost everyone was out of town. Beatrice was in Shelburne, but I saw Amy [Bend], and she dined with us Wednesday evening. We stopped at the Waldorf. J was in town and came to see me in the afternoon and dined with us. In a certain way it seemed so natural to see him again, and in another way queer. He comes up here on Friday. I am wild for it, the rides and talks and drives and walks. Louis Webb and Mr. Hoyt came back with us; Uncle Willie gave up his trip on the yacht at the last minute, and he and Mr. Beach returned to Paris. Louis spoke several times of Mr. Beach but only the first days, for I never brought up the subject though I wanted to often, but it was better not.

Sunday, June 17.

J arrived Friday morning. This morning he has come down with the mumps! It is pathetically ludicrous that one minute I feel like crying and the next like laughing. His father and brother had it two weeks ago, and yesterday he told me that one side of his face felt queer and hurt, and I promptly said we would try mind-curing it, but it hasn't worked. Poor thing, he has fever and feels wretchedly today. Fortunately Dr. McLane is stopping with us so he could attend to him at once. He said that none of us could see him for a week. What a long dreary week for him. Mamma has written to ask Mrs. Burden to come here for a few days because J will be so lonely, and besides, Mrs. Burden will probably worry. It is really hard luck. The last time we were going to say goodbye to each other he had the measles; this time it is the mumps.

The Burdens all sail for Europe in two weeks so he will only just be well in time. I am horribly disappointed myself and probably show it in my face, for the remarks of the family generally have been most amusing. Grandma and Aunt Maggie Bromley are with us, and the latter of course is always joking. Today at luncheon Mamma was reading in a letter from some friend that Prince Joseph of Battenberg had liked me so much in Paris, and I said quickly "Ah, yes! He was so interesting. I shall be glad to see him again." Whereupon Aunt Maggie calmly remarked that she thought it was very safe for me to meet foreigners now, for I was in no danger of being attracted in that direction!

The two days with J were perfect days; we rode and

walked and spent one morning on the lake, and talked, talked without stopping and without caring to stop. I have missed him frightfully today, and I shall go on missing him every day.

Seward came down for two days last week, and we had a good many talks together. He has sent me my saddle horse, but I have not ridden her yet.

The Shepards sailed for Europe on Wednesday to be gone all summer.

Sunday, *11* P.M., *June 24*.

I do not feel like going to bed, and I do not feel like writing, and thinking makes me excited and nervous, and reading is out of the question. Of all, writing is the easiest, and it may have a quieting effect on my nerves. Somehow or other I don't quite understand or remember that J has told me that he likes me and that I have said "yes" to him, and that he has held me in his arms and kissed me, and that I have kissed him often. But we are not going to speak of any binding promise or anything like an engagement until this fall. Both of us are to have our summer absolutely free: I to live my life as I please, he to live his as he pleases, and then, after the summer is over, we will speak of the seriousness of all this, if in the meantime neither of us have changed. I do care for him very much; I want to care a great deal more. I feel sure that he cares for me, not in the way Mr. Beach did, and not in the way Mr. Whitehouse does, with an almost foolish adoration, but with a caring based on friendship, sympathy, and mutual interest. I am glad about it, very, very glad and happy. He has been laid up all the week with his mumps, but since Wednesday I have gone and sat outside on the windowsill of his room, and we have talked together by the hour and also read aloud. Today for the first time we took a walk together. What a perfect afternoon it has been! And this evening sitting in the billiard room with him. Neither of us are going to speak of this to a soul. It would make us seem less free if we did, and that of all things I want to be yet a while.

Wednesday, June 27.

J left last evening. I did not know that it would be so hard to have him go, so hard to say goodbye. But it was horribly hard, and today I feel lonely and more or less blue and depressed. Each day this week with him has been more perfect than the last, and I have been with him every minute.

14

Jay's Courtship

J Burden was in Europe with his family for four months, beginning in July of 1894. He and Adele had come to an understanding before he left: they were in love but not engaged, devoted but not bound. And it was all to be kept the strictest secret, although Adele was to have the privilege of reassuring her family that he was "serious." It was taken for granted that they would correspond by every steamer.

They agreed that social life for each should continue as usual, but Adele had not anticipated that J would enjoy it quite so much or be quite so candid about it. The whirl of Scottish house parties was "go, go, go," he wrote her, and she was less than pleased. J, however, at last got the idea and began to concentrate in his letters on how much he missed her. He described a visit to a famous palmist and mind reader in London and enclosed the scrap of paper on which the seer had spelled out, through thought transmission, the name of his beloved. And when he went to Cowes on board *The Whyte Lady*, the yacht of the Ogden Goelets, he was careful to poke fun at Mrs. Goelet's pretty but tuft-hunting younger sister Grace Wilson who was scanning the Solent for dukes.

This same Grace was in two years' time to marry Adele's cousin Cornelius Vanderbilt III, over the violent opposition of his family. Neither her beauty nor her fortune nor her social

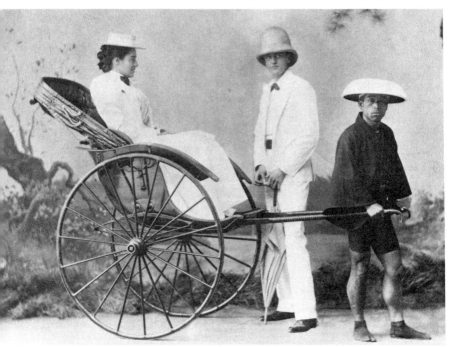

Adele and J on their honeymoon, in Japan, 1895.

connections could compensate for the embarrassment she caused them by the brainless exuberance with which she made a farce of the social game.

J's letters to Adele show a very serious and literal young man, very much in love. He was extremely conservative, even for his era, and felt that it was incumbent upon him to correct Adele's "socialist tendencies" by stressing the importance in Europe—and particularly in so volatile a nation as France—of strong government to avoid "riots." But for all this gravity, one is struck by the fun the young couple had in keeping their "secret" from the world. J's letters are filled with speculations as to who has "guessed" or not guessed. This went on for months, without apparently ever boring him or Adele. J describes with obvious satisfaction how his mother keeps peeking at him to see if his expression, when not watched, may not reveal something of the state of his heart. And even after the Burdens' return to New York, he refused to allay his father's natural anxiety that he might be "flirting" reprehensibly with Miss Sloane, thereby giving rise to serious misapprehensions in her parents, until he had Adele's permission to announce their troth.

It all seems a bit quaint in the light of the sexual revolution of our times, but who is to say which generation had the more fun?

15

The Diary:
July 1 to December 31, 1894

Elm Court, Lenox. Sunday, July 1.

I had a telegram from J yesterday just before he went aboard the *Lucania*, and he has written to me each day since he left, and I to him, and it will seem so long now to wait for his next letter, unless I get one by the pilot. I told Mamma and Papa about him the other day, and I never saw people more absolutely glad about a thing. And it is delightful to hear Grandma and Aunt Maggie Bromley rave over him, and everyone else say such lovely things. He really is too dear, and I can't say how happy I am about it all. God keep him safely on this journey. I am loving him more and more each day. I am sorry I have said that so often before in my life, but for the time it was true, and in the first case, it certainly did not hurt me. On the contrary, it helped me above all things to grow. In the second case, it was, as I said all along, an intense excitement, a thing of the senses, not of the soul. It was a mistake, and I not only hurt the man but myself as well. I am sorry for it, and I have suffered. I told J about it, and I did not tell him about the first thing. Some day I will; it is better never to have anything underneath, but all on the surface.[1] I feel as if I did not deserve this happiness at all; I have done nothing to bring it on, but I shall try now, oh so hard, to be worthy of it!

Friday, July 6.

I am having a very queer little private attack of the mumps. No one knows anything about it but Emily and Edith Knowlton. It began last Saturday. Monday I felt wretchedly and had an awful headache which gave me the excuse of staying in bed. There was not much swelling in my face, but it hurt, and I am sure I had fever. Tuesday I kept quiet and Wednesday felt almost all right again. But today the swelling has gone down in my throat in small hard lumps, and it is anything but comfortable. How the family would laugh if they knew it! Or worry? I only hope I am not giving it to any of them. I could not help but have it. I used to sit on the windowsill in J's room for hours every day, and I cannot say that he was ever at a very safe distance. It was generally on a chair close to the window, with both my hands in his, while I read aloud. Oh, how I wish I could have it over again. Such a dear letter came from him by the pilot; I still write every day and send the letters twice a week.

I hope these horrid mumps will soon disappear; they make me feel rather forlorn. Papa informed me that I looked thin and pale and has made me begin a tonic. I have not energy enough to ride, but yesterday I drove the brake for an hour and a half and later tried a new pair of horses Papa has bought for Emily and me. The weather is beautiful; I only hope it will keep so next week when Harry Whitney comes.

Sunday evening, July 8.

Unfortunately my poor little mumps is no longer private property. The swelling in my throat had increased so by Saturday and was so painful that I had to tell the family. The doctor came over later and told me that, of course, I must not

[1] A bit disingenuous? J must have heard about Freddy Beach, but did not perhaps know about Gifford Pinchot.

move out of my room, and I have my face all bandaged up and feel like a forlorn wretch. It hurts more today than it did yesterday, and it is almost impossible to chew anything. J will feel so terribly when he knows about it; I am writing him, however, not to waste any pity on me when he reads the letter because by that time I shall probably be entirely well and quite forgetting these long dreary days all alone in my room. Fortunately I have no headache, so I can read to my heart's content though my eyes are already beginning to feel the effect of it. All last week's supposed mumps were really only a leading up to it. It takes about ten days to develop; I only hope none of the rest of the family will take it, though it is rather a joke on me.

Friday, July 20.

Harry left today; he has been here since Monday, and I wanted him so much to stay over Sunday, but he had asked some fellows to come to him at Roslyn, so he had to leave. I have indeed made up this week for last week's long dreary days. It has been very warm, but Harry and I rode for two and three hours every afternoon, going out at five o'clock and coming home a few minutes before eight. It was perfect, and I enjoyed our talks as much as I always do. We went out for several moonlight walks together, but the talk never approached anything in the way of sentimentality. I am more than glad for Harry's friendship and shall try hard all my life to keep it. Charlie Sands and George Dyer arrive this evening. Mr. [Benoni] Lockwood telegraphed that on account of his father's illness it would be impossible for him to come; I am disappointed.

Two long letters have come from J, the first one from Queenstown, thirty-six pages, the second from London, twenty-four pages. I look forward to each steamer. I am thinking all the time of this last thing in my life, thinking, wondering and praying over it. God help me to do what is right and best, best for me, best for him, and help me to know and be sure of myself. There are times when the questions and doubts will come up, and when I am nervous and unhappy. Is it always so? Sometimes I feel so very sure and so very glad, if it could only always be that way.

Pointe d'Acadie,[2] *Bar Harbor. Sunday, August 5.*
We arrived here on Wednesday. I love the place, the water, the bracing air, the whole feeling of it. I wish J were here, wish it with a great tremendous wish. What fun to go off in the water with him, to take long walks back in the woods up the mountains, long drives. I should love it, love it. His letters come twice a week, and mine go out twice a week. He misses me, but he is having a splendid time; I miss him but am quite contented and happy living the life I am living. Does that sound all right? Are the days over when the sun looks dark and the skies dreary, and the birds' songs [sound] sad because the loved one is away? I wonder; it seems to me that the more I loved the happier and gladder I would be. My life would seem fuller, the world larger and more crowded with interest and beauty. Is the time gone by when one's life, especially a woman's life, was small and narrow, and then love came and took absolute possession of it, and the few other things were crowded out, and its whole force was concentrated in one object—and then the absence of that object meant misery? Is it so to such a degree now? For myself I cannot understand it. I have resources; I have my books, my thoughts, my love of physical life and enjoyments; I am happy alone. I can be infinitely more happy with the person I love, and have vastly more pleasure and interest—what I mean is that the other is not negative, and I cannot conceive of its being so.

Last Sunday I was in Beverly Farms with Mary Andrews. We had four perfect days together, talking from morning till night. I am glad that none of my strong friendships have ever grown any less.

Bar Harbor is just the same as ever; one sees about the same people, and the same number of dances and dinners and picnics are being given. I dined at the Kebo Club last evening with the Coles and stayed afterward for the dance. It was rather amusing, but I do not know many of the people. I see

[2] George Vanderbilt's house on Mount Desert Island, Maine.

the Palmers every day and have heard Courtlandt play by the hour; it is absolute enjoyment. He is coming here for all this afternoon.

Newport. Sunday, August 19.

A year ago from today I was here having very much the same kind of a time as I am having this year but enjoying it in a totally different kind of way. I never shall forget the wild enthusiasm I brought into everything I did last summer and the intense excitement of it all. I wish I could bring it back again but I can't. Emily and I came here on Wednesday from Bar Harbor and are stopping with the Cornelius Vanderbilts.[3] I have been in a rush every minute. The things I have enjoyed most so far have been a drive out to Tiverton the other evening in Seward's [Seward Webb] coach, dinner there, and the drive back at midnight by moonlight. He had Mr. and Mrs. J. J. Astor, Mrs. Ladenburg, Beatrice [Bend], Mr. and Mrs. Courtlandt Palmer, and Howard Cushing and myself. I sat in the back seat going out with Howard Cushing. He is interesting and attractive. Perry Belmont also drove his coach out with Mr. and Mrs. Whitney Waire, Mr. and Mrs. Jimmy Lanier, Baron Fallon and Count Lienstaff. At dinner I sat next to Mr. Belmont and had the nicest talk I have ever had with him. After dinner he took me out in a rowboat for an hour. How perfect it is to be on the water in a little boat following the silver sparkling path which the moon makes and listening to the dip of the oars and the drip and soft splash of the water. I loved it. Seward took me out two other times in his coach, and once I drove the whole way myself.

The other thing I have enjoyed was last night in the [Elbridge] Gerrys' yacht. It was very much the same kind of a night as last year. A full moon, a clear sky, and fleecy floating clouds. In all other respects it was different. I did not have a person at my feet adoring me, so to speak, but rather amusing uninteresting talks, the first part of the evening with Charlie Sands, the second part with Dick Wilson. The latter

3 The Cornelius Vanderbilts' great Newport villa, The Breakers, was not completed until 1895, so presumably they were renting this summer.

was up in Bar Harbor the four days before I left, and I saw him often. He had a very jolly dinner of sixteen at the Malvern one night, and I sat one side of him and later, out on the piazza, star gazing for an hour. He is silly and makes me often angry at myself and angry at him, but in certain ways I like him.

Friday night Mrs. [Ogden] Mills had a cotillion. I danced with Seward and went into supper with Reggie Ronalds. It was nice and I enjoyed myself, but these sorts of things seem so out of place in the summer time. Yesterday was the coach parade. Seward, in Perry Belmont's coach; he had Mr. and Mrs. Bayard Cutting, Angelica Gerry, and Bert Robbins. We all drove out to the Golf Club, lunched there, and came home at five o'clock. Tomorrow Aunt Alice [Vanderbilt] has a big picnic out at the Farm. Seward, Mr. Belmont, Mr. Mills, and Mr. Bronson take their coaches. I am sure it will be great fun. We are to be here until Friday and then go back to Lenox, and I don't want to go away again until the second week in November. I had forty pages from J the other day in two long interesting letters. I count the days for his letters and more than ever love them.

Elm Court, Lenox. Sunday August 26.

Emily and I came back here from Newport on Friday and brought Beatrice with us. It is so perfect having her here. What a thing friendship is, how it gives the heart and soul a stir-up. I could not have a more perfect friend than Beatrice is. People say that women are incapable of friendship. What perfect trash and nonsense! They are capable of just as true and great a friendship as men. It does not come nearly as often, but when it does come, it is just the same in intensity and degree. I think Beatrice and I have been through a strong enough test; it is what would break up in a minute a weak friendship, but what makes a strong one infinitely stronger. I could not get on without her help and trust and sympathy. We are to be alone together for a week; then a number of men come up for next Sunday. I saw Harry Whitney the last two days in Newport; it was so nice seeing him again. He is coming here on Friday. I was not sorry to leave Newport but, on the contrary, glad; of course, for the time being I enjoyed it as one always does that kind of excitement. Of the new people I met, I like Mr. Cottenet[4] best and hope to know him some day. Mamma said she would ask him up here.

Sunday, September 2.

Mr. Lockwood, Charlie Sands, Harry Whitney, and Uncle Henry [Sloane] are here. We had such a long delightful day yesterday. In the morning I took the brake out, and we all went for an hour and a half's drive, Harry and I taking turns driving. In the afternoon four of us rode and two drove over to Stevens Glen and had an hour's picnic there with chicken and jam sandwiches, cake, and fruit. It was so jolly. I rode both ways with Mr. Lockwood; it is nice seeing him again and I am glad that I like him. Last night Beatrice and I played jokes and carried on from twelve o'clock until one, ringing bells, throwing wet towels, etc., and behaving generally like perfect children. The rain still does not come, and the country looks burnt and dried up, and the roads are thick in dust. J writes such enthusiastic letters about Scotland. How many times I wish I were there with him!

Thursday, September 6.

I feel in quite a lonely dreary mood with everyone gone. Beatrice left yesterday and the men on Tuesday. We kept up a succession of childish games and teasings. I do not think I have ever carried on as much in my life. Sunday afternoon in Cozy Cot we were all terrible, threw powder and sugar at each other, to say nothing of water, upset tables and chairs and were like wild Indians for two hours. But that sort of thing does one good once in a while. One never can force oneself to be like a child, and when it comes naturally, it is delicious. Beatrice and I wrote Harry a killing letter the day he left. I suppose by this time he has gotten it. I wish I could see the expression on his face as he read it. I have never seen him in a better spirit than he was here, and Mr. Lockwood and he

4 Rawlins Cottenet, who managed The Rosary, a fashionable flower shop in New York.

kept us in gales of laughter the entire time. Mr. Lockwood
comes up again tomorrow for Sunday. I only wish Beatrice
and Harry were also coming.

Wednesday, September 19.

My twenty-first birthday! How old and dignified that
sounds, not nearly as nice as twenty. I am fearfully sorry to
have this year ended, it is and has been such a full one. How
different it all is today from this time last year; it makes me
horribly quiet and depressed when I think of it all. I have not
by any means put it entirely out of my life yet; one does not
immediately jump out of those sorts of things. I wonder how
it will be next year! Very different or just the same as it is
now?

We have had a lot of people in the house over Sunday, and
I have enjoyed it, but for some reason or other I have not
been in good spirits, except when I have been riding and then
I forget everything. Mr. [Jim] Appleton and I have been for
long rides every day, and we planned the longest one for
today; only unfortunately it is raining, with no prospect of
clearing.

Sunday, September 30.

Mr. Cottenet has been here since Thursday. I like him thoroughly and am quite excited at the thought of having made a
new friend; they are so few and far between just at present. I
have been spending the afternoon in Cozy Cot with him, talking for two hours and reading Buckle[5] for one hour. We built
a fire, and at first I felt rather blue sitting there as I used to
last year. He spoke about Mr. [Freddy] Beach and how much
he liked him, and as usual I was glad; I always am glad when
people praise him. Then he spoke about Harry and how much
better Harry had always like me than any other girl and how
nice it would have been if he were older, etc., etc. I have
asked him to come up again in October and shall try and per-
suade Harry to come the same time.

[5] Henry Thomas Buckle, a British historian, whose writings were widely
discussed at this time.

We have had two glorious long rides together. The weather is changing into cold, short autumn days when the air is intoxicatingly full of life, and one feels quite drunk with the beauty of everything. Mrs. Murray, Miss Frelinghuysen, Theodore [Frelinghuysen], Esther Hunt, and Meredith Howland are with us, but I have not seen much of anyone but Mr. Cottenet, although Esther Hunt rather surprised me today by saying such lovely things to me. I must be a very queer mixture of a lot of different things. I wish I could be an outsider and see myself for a little while—how funny it would be.

J writes that he is not coming home until November.[6] I am very disappointed for I want to see him here and not in New York. I do not want to have anything decided between us yet —I am not half sure enough of myself—and I do not think he is either—but these sorts of things are so much more easily talked about when one has long uninterrupted days. I hate the little short city talks.

Tuesday, October 2.

More wonderfully beautiful days! How much longer is this weather going to last? I got up early yesterday morning and breakfasted at quarter before seven with Mr. Cottenet and Mr. Howland, and then because it was so glorious out, I could not resist the temptation of driving down to the station with them. I wish I could enjoy those early morning hours much oftener; they give me such a well, happy feeling to begin the day with. I am sorry Mr. Cottenet has gone, and I quite miss my long hours with him.

A letter from Harry came this morning, the first one since he left; such a nice letter. I do hope he will come up with Mr. Cottenet by the eighteenth. I wish he were here today to go for a long, long ride with me. I went with Mr. Frelinghuysen yesterday, and we were gone for almost three hours. Coming home the sunset almost drove me crazy, a great golden red sky, a tiny silver moon, and a star to wish by. Mrs. Mills and

[6] J had graduated from Harvard College in the spring of 1893 and, after a year at Harvard Law School, had started working at the Burden ironworks in Troy in May 1894.

Kitty Havemeyer have both asked me to stop with them this
month, but it is so hard to get away from here that I regret-
ted. In a certain way it would have been fun.

Esther Hunt is with me very much, the way May Palmer
was in Bar Harbor. It always strikes me as being rather funny,
though I have so often loved women myself when they have
only cared very little for me; but with girls somehow it seems
different, and I feel rather piggishly selfish at being told how
much I am cared for, etc., and saying nothing in return.
Esther is Emily's friend, and I did not know her at all before
she came here, but she informed me yesterday that she loved
me infinitely more than she did Emily and then said a lot of
other things, among them the usual remarks of strangers to
me, namely, that I am frightfully cold and indifferent and un-
get-at-able. Am I? It seems to me that I am just the opposite; I
give out too much sympathy and care too much, and have to
suffer in consequence.

Mr. Crosby was here for four days; he left yesterday. He
dined with us twice and yesterday morning we took a walk of
two hours together. He tires me infinitely and still, because I
have liked him, I want to be nice to him, and I always stand
up for him if anyone runs him down; but he does not interest
me in the tiniest degree, and we have very little in sympathy
to talk about.

Thursday, October 11.

Is it only my imagination or is it true? For somehow or other,
J's letters have seemed different lately. One came this morning, and I have it before me now. There is nothing about
coming home or wanting to come home in it. Nothing about
missing me, or thinking of me, but raving about his perfect
time in Scotland, about the big house parties at Mrs. Martin's
where he has been stopping, of the different people who have
asked him to visit them, how he wished he had more time to
pay these visits, etc., etc. Of course, it is all very natural, but
would it be quite the same if he felt the same for me as he did
when he left here? I doubt it. J is very attractive, and he is
finding that out more and more all the time, and finding out

his power to make people like him. He ought to know and feel it now; it is dangerous when it comes later in a man's life, when he no longer has the freedom to use it. I know how I felt last summer when it first took hold of me, and this last week I have been living over again every day of last year at this time, knowing and remembering so well the excitement and happiness of it all. Would I care very much if J changed? Yes, I am sure I would; it would hurt frightfully, but would it be my pride or my love that was most hurt? I think, my love first and through that my pride. But why ask all these questions? I am blue and rather down in the mouth, and it is a bad time to put my feeling on paper. Will I laugh at them in a month?

Tuesday, October 16.

I have decided after all to go to Mrs. Mills [at Staatsburg][7] this week. She telegraphed me on Sunday asking me to change my mind and come. So I am going down tomorrow morning with the Mortons and stop with them for a day, and then to Mrs. Mills on Thursday. She has a dance Friday night and a golf tournament on Saturday. I am sure a few days of that life will be great fun, and I am looking forward to it. Also I am looking forward to having a nice talk with Mr. [Alfred] Coats, whom I met the other day and liked. He is a great friend of J's. I still keep hearing things about J all the time. Of his being devoted enough to some English girl to be reported engaged. Of what a flirt he was, etc., etc. I wrote him the other day that I wanted him to tell me before he saw me whether he had changed or not. I feel almost sure that he has.

We have had a delightful house party over Sunday. The Whitelaw Reids, Loulie Baylies, Edith and Lena Morton, Mr. Depew,[8] Theodore Frelinghuysen, the Fred Baldwins, Mrs. Gregory, and Charlie Robinson. Sunday afternoon Walter Damrosch was here, and he played Wagner for us over an

---

[7] Mrs. Ogden Mills (Ruth Livingston), whose house on the Hudson River, at Staatsburg, New York, just north of Hyde Park, was reputedly the model for the Trenors' in Edith Wharton's *The House of Mirth*.
[8] Chauncey Depew, the general counsel of the Vanderbilt railroads and a noted wit and public speaker.

hour; it could not have been more delightful. We are going to drive over to Lebanon today and take luncheon there. The weather has gotten very cold; we actually had a little snow the other afternoon, and there are heavy frosts every night.

Sunday, October 21.

I have been in a perfect rush since Wednesday, but such a delightful rush. I am sorry it is over. I left Wednesday with the Mortons, spent that night with them, drove the next afternoon with Edith, Lena, and Beatrice Bend to Staatsburg. Mrs. Mills had just come in from playing golf when we arrived. As it was only five o'clock, with the prospect of a glorious sunset on the river, she suggested going out in the launch and getting Mr. Hoyt to take us, which we promptly did. It could not have been nicer, and Mrs. Mills was a revelation to me. It shows what a terrible mistake [it is] to judge of people only by hearsay. We got back at half past six, had tea in the hall, talked till seven, and then went upstairs to dress. That evening there were only Mrs. Billy Travers, Anna Sands, Mr. Hoyt, Mr. Cary, Mrs. Mills, and myself for dinner, so we had a quiet time and I went to bed at half past ten.

The next day Friday was gloriously beautiful. I took a three hours' drive with Seward who had arrived that morning, got back in time for luncheon which we took in his car. That afternoon I spent most of my time sitting on the piazza jabbering at a tremendous rate to different people. There were thirty-three people for dinner that evening. I sat between Dick Wilson and Mr. Bodkin, and after dinner was blissfully happy with Beatrice. The cotillion began at a little after half past ten. I danced with Reggie Ronalds. Seward had asked me, and Mr. Coats said he had wanted to. I had much my nicest talk of the evening with him, or rather talks. I was crazy to ask him to come up here for next Sunday but determined that I had better not. I like him and I am sure I shall go on liking him more and more.

I never enjoyed a dance more than I did that one, for I never felt more in the spirit of a thing. It was perfect enjoyment from beginning to end. I must confess I went out on the piazza quite often, but that was the fault of the night and not mine; the moon and the stars were too enticingly beautiful to resist and the still cold air too delicious not to long for. Worthy asked me to go out with him for a little while; he began talking to me again in exactly the same old way. I wonder why. He was here with us for several days this autumn and never referred to anything. I was glad because I was sure he had gotten over it. But he told me over and over again that night that he never would get over it; instead of loving me less, he kept on loving me more and more all the time. I wonder what I ought to do. He told me that it never entered his head that I could care for him, so I must do nothing whatever about it. I feel so frightfully sorry for him.

The dance was kept going until three o'clock. I woke up the next morning feeling wretchedly ill, gave as an excuse the fact of having caught a heavy cold the previous night and it would be impossible for me to leave my room all day. I saw no one but Mrs. Mills, Beatrice, and Seward. The latter was too angelic and suggested taking me in his [private railroad] car that night and bringing me here. I dreaded spending another day there in bed, so selfishly said yes. Seward is really too lovely to me. He brought me all the way to Pittsfield, sidetracked his car so I would not have to get up until late this morning, saw me in the carriage, and then went all that extra distance back to Shelburne.

I found a large box of the most beautiful roses from Mr. Cottenet waiting for me here. I can't get over his having sent them; it is so nice. I am looking forward to seeing him on Friday. There were also two letters for me from J, lovely letters, but still the something wanting in them. Will that same something be wanting in him when I see him?

Thursday evening, October 25.

Mr. Cottenet telegraphed me two days ago saying that it would be impossible for him to come here tomorrow on account of important business, and yesterday I had such a nice letter from him. I am very disappointed. Mamma wrote Mr. Coats asking him to come, but I am afraid it was too short a notice.

There was no letter today from J. Somehow or other I have a horrid hurt feeling through me lately. I am afraid I shall care a great deal more than I thought I would if he has changed toward me. I do not believe that he likes anyone else; I only think he likes me a great deal less and rather dreads the thought of feeling perhaps that he will have to bind himself to some promise. That certainly will not be the case; I do not want a binding promise any more than he does. I will have to trust him a great deal more and be a great deal surer of myself than now. It is only a little over two weeks before I expect to see him. There are so few more chances for him to write that I was more than disappointed when no letter came today by the *Majestic*.

Sunday, October 28.

A letter from J came yesterday, still without any mention of sailing. He was stopping with the Cravens. He told me that he had a very exciting, interesting experience to relate to me. I suppose some friends want him to live over there, or some one friend wants to marry him, or something like that. What a lot of things he will have to tell me when I see' him; unfortunately I rather dread some of the things. It has been perfectly glorious out all yesterday and today. If Mr. Cottenet had been here, what delightful rides and walks we could have had. Two such nice letters have come from him this week. It is only four days before I leave; as usual, it makes me ill to think of it. I am more than dreading certain things in the city.

New York. Saturday evening, November 10.

J is home; he came to see me this afternoon and stayed two hours. Has he changed or hasn't he? I do not know. I was more than glad to see him, and I scarcely stopped to think if he was as glad to see me or not. I am quite sure that he has not the faintest idea of what it is to be really in love. Unfortunately, I can draw a number of comparisons in my mind. I know very well what it is to be really loved and having once known a strong man's real love, nothing short of it would ever satisfy me. I think J probably would like to go on this winter just like he did last, see a lot of me and enjoy a delightful *bonne camaraderie*. But that is impossible. I am not going to let people talk about me and gossip the way they did last year; as I said before, I have got to draw a narrower line of conventionality than I have been used to. J is coming to spend all tomorrow afternoon with me. I must begin soon and say no to all those things he asks me to do. He has decided to spend most of the winter in Troy.

I enjoyed my short visit at Tuxedo very much. The Mortimers had Mr. Crosby and Dick Wilson stopping in the house at the same time. I wish Dick Wilson would not affect quite such a devoted manner to me as he has adopted for the present; it irritates me and makes me angry with myself and with him. Mr. Cottenet came to Tuxedo for a few hours to arrange the flowers at the club the night of the dance. He wrote me that he had only come in to see me. Such a pretty little speech!

Last night I dined in at George's. Richard [Harding] Davis took me in, and Courtlandt Palmer was on the other side, so I had a most enjoyable evening.

I feel like writing a lot more about J and myself and several mixed up things, but am too tired to sit up any longer.

Shelburne Farms. Thursday, November 22.

How different it has all been here from what it was last year. Just a year ago today I was writing in this journal. I have not changed so tremendously. I know myself almost as little and my future just as little as I did then. Creighton [Webb] talked to me the other night till I almost cried. He said I had no idea of responsibility and no idea of what it was to ruin people's lives. He told me I had ruined his and ruined Mr. Beach's and that I was heartless enough to start ahead and ruin J Burden's. It is untrue, absolutely untrue. Creighton never could have thought that there was the slightest chance of my ever caring for him; at least, I do not see how he ever could have, although he says now that he did, and it is the only thing he has been working for for the last two years, the only reason he took up work at all and went to Russia. I can't begin to say all the things he told me. He never spoke that way in Paris, never half as strongly or as seriously.

J was here over Sunday. I want to be with him. I want him to love me, and I want to love him. How will it all come out in the end? God only knows. I don't want to make any more mistakes or hurt any more people or hurt myself. It is always just as difficult to unmake a reputation as to make it. If people get it into their heads that one is supposed to be attractive, or wishes to flirt, they start in with that idea and are much nicer to you for the time being than they otherwise would have been. I am not foolish enough to say that I don't want to be liked, because I do want it, but there is a limit at which the line must be drawn. I more than detest that people should simply shrug their shoulders and laugh and say, "Oh, yes! But then she is such a flirt." It is so horribly undignified and makes me feel as mean as dirt.

New York. Friday evening, November 30.

I have just been spending two such delightful days at Roslyn with the Whitneys and only wish I could have stayed over Sunday. Yesterday morning Harry let me ride his hunter, Bene Hassan, and we took a two hours' ride across the plains, half the time at a mad tear. It was splendid and makes my blood tingle even now to think of it. We stopped in for a few minutes at Mr. Cottenet's, and he took me through his greenhouse and cut me one of the most beautiful American beauties I have ever seen; it stood six feet from the ground. I have it by me now. I like him just as much as I did at first, in fact better, and I thoroughly enjoy talking to him. I wish the Whitneys did not sail on Wednesday; Harry is such a delightful person to get up a lot of schemes with. He does not seem to want to go at all. I have not seen J yet; he comes to town tomorrow so as to be here for the games. I am going on Reggie Ronalds' party which the Astors are chaperoning, Gertrude [Vanderbilt], Edith Morton and myself, Mr. Taylor,

Mr. Cottenet, Mr. Coats, Lorie Ronalds, and I believe one or two others. If it is only a pleasant day we will have such fun.

Thursday, December 6.

My mind at present is pretty much taken up with one subject, namely, J. I am beginning to want him more and more all the time, to miss him fearfully when he is away, and to be perfectly happy when he is with me. I am very sure that he loves me, but just how much I don't know. I am very sure, too, that I love him, but how much, time will have to show. He was here last Saturday and Sunday, and we were together most of the time. He writes to me every day and I to him. He said in his last letter that he could not help but feel that we belong to each other. In a way I think we do; I think one day we will entirely. No wonder all my thinking is done in this line! We had a dance Tuesday night over in the picture gallery.[9] It was great fun. Some people thought it was given for the purpose of announcing my engagement to J. I was informed of the fact often during the evening. What idiots people are! I should think they would be busy enough with their own lives without looking after other people.

I was at the Palmers' all yesterday afternoon listening to Courtlandt play. He sent me the most beautiful basket of orchids I have ever seen the evening of our dance, and Mr. Cottenet sent me eight of his enormous American beauties. I have begun my riding in town, and although it makes me long more than ever for the country, it is better than nothing. Both Mr. Appleton and Mr. Cottenet have asked me to ride with them, and every Saturday that I can, I am going with J.

Friday, 6:15 P.M., *December 7.*

I have just been having a very disagreeable fight with myself, and am at present trying to feel satisfied that I have decided right. It is church night and as usual we are all expected to go, and as usual I do not want to, but up till this afternoon thought nothing about it excepting that it was my duty to go.

[9] At 640 Fifth Avenue, residence of Adele's grandmother Mrs. William H. Vanderbilt.

However, at luncheon Beatrice begged me to go to the opera
with her this evening, and I have just had a note from J this
morning telling me that he would be down for it and would
look forward to seeing me there. Of course I want to go, and
told Beatrice I would, persuading myself that going to church
in a rebellious, discontented frame of mind would do me no
good whatever—in fact, hurt me. I came home and told this
to Mother, and she said if J felt this way, of course, I could go
with the Bends, but that she felt very badly about it, although
she would not dream of asking me to go to church simply to
please her. Whereupon I came back to my room and the fight
inside began. Then all of a sudden such a wave of beastly
selfishness came over me that I sat down and wrote Beatrice I
could not come. It hadn't been a question all along of right
and wrong but simply of what I wanted to do and what I
ought to do. Whether church does me any good or right tonight, I think the struggle has, although I wish I could feel a
little more contented about it.

LATER. No, church did not do a particle of good. Even
Mother said she would not ask me to go again. It was so long
and tiresome and uninteresting and I could not get the feeling
out of me that I wanted to be at the opera and had made a stupid decision. I want to see J.

Wednesday, December 12.

Since I last wrote I feel as if I had crossed a wide boundary
line and come out on the other side. It isn't theory or talk any
more; J does love me, and I love him in a deep, serious, earnest
way, and we are going to spend all our lives together. God
grant that we may never hurt each other in any way. No one
knows of this yet; we almost have not had time to know it
ourselves. But it is true, and I feel it more and more all the
time.

Today Uncle Willie and Mr. Beach arrive home. Perhaps I
will see Mr. Beach at the opera tonight. I feel like being a
coward and staying home. I do not believe at all the stories
people tell about him, and I wish I could stand up for him

Adele and J at the time of their engagement, 1895.

more than ever. But I can't, I can't say anything. He will not want to see me or talk to me, and if he did the conversation would be horribly strained. The last time we talked together I promised that I would try and love him. I don't want to excuse myself in the least degree. I have said over and over again that the whole thing was a mistake. I have suffered for the mistake. I probably will feel frightfully when I see him now, but I cannot undo the wrong I did, the wrong which hurt him even more than it did me. He is only going to be here a short while and then starts off again with Uncle Willie for the East.

Aunt Alva is getting a divorce from Uncle Willie, and none of the family see her, and consequently the children either. I am sure Consuelo must feel very badly about it.

Sunday evening, December 16.

I have given J my solemn promise that I would marry him. Yesterday it was, but somehow it seems much longer ago. I have thought of it so much that the feeling that I belong to him has almost become natural. I do love him with all my heart, and I want to spend all my life with him. It does not seem queer; on the contrary, it strikes me as being very natural. We have been so much together for the last year and have grown so into each other's lives that the thought of always going on this way is much easier to believe than the thought of its ever stopping. I am very sure that it is right and true, surer than I have ever been of anything in my life; I can't explain why, but I am.

We are not going to tell anyone yet, not even Papa and Mamma for just this week. Only Fred Winthrop knows; J told him today. I do not think people will be at all surprised when we announce our engagement; it has been spoken about so much already and has even been dragged through the papers this last week.

I am very happy, and I know he is too. I am sure that neither of us are doing this without having thought very seriously and very long about it. It is much the greatest, most solemn step in one's life. I have been near making mistakes before; I have done lots of crazy things. God help me always in the future to be perfectly true to the promise I made J yesterday—and keep him true to his.

Sunday, 11:30 P.M., December 23.

I am absolutely happy, happier than I had any idea the word meant. It is all true; I do love him and he loves me and we belong to each other for all our lives. His mother came to see me today, and she was too sweet with me. He only told her yesterday. I told Mother on Wednesday. Everyone is glad. I am glad myself, oh, so glad! I am living in the highest strain of

Adele (left) and J (right), with Gertrude and Harry Whitney at the latter's house on October Mountain, Massachusetts, 1896.

excitement all the time. It is impossible to put things into words. He has just left, and I must go over again to myself all this perfect day with him.

Monday night, 11:45 P.M., December 31.

There are just a few minutes left of the old year, and I must write a word in my journal before it closes. It is the last year of my life spent only for myself, the last year that I shall be quite the independent Adele Sloane. Am I sorry? No, I could not wish it to be this way any more. I must belong to J. I want to spend all my life with him. I could not stand it any different way now. The bells are beginning to ring. I thank God for another perfectly happy year.

Adele and J, June 6, 1895.

16

Weddings in the Nineties

Nothing is more striking to today's reader of Adele's journal than the fact that she hardly ever mentions money. Even in her cousin Gertrude's diary there is no emphasis on it—she complains bitterly about the problems created for romance by the label "heiress" that is tied around her neck, but she does not tell her reader who has money or where it came from. Yet this should not be taken as evidence that money was not important to the two diarists. On the contrary, it was built into the very soul of the society in which the cousins grew up. It may even not be fanciful to suggest that, like a religious mystery, it was too sacred to be carelessly profaned.

My mother, who was a little girl in the 1890s, used to tell me of a worldly old grandmother of hers whose flat, trenchant statements about the value of money were deplored by the more delicate-minded members of the family. "Do not speak ill of Mrs. Kingsland," she told Mother once. "She has three million dollars." Now this was certainly crass, but crass people have a way of expressing what the rest of us will not admit, even to ourselves. The society of which that long row of derivative châteaux running up Fifth Avenue was the ultimate architectural expression was as material as any society since that of Rome under the Antonines, and the row of portrait busts from the latter era in the Louvre, substituting frock coats for togas, could pass for corporate directors in the lobby of any firm in Wall Street.

Money has had its place in the societies and courts of most nations, but it has usually been tempered with other elements, such as birth or military prowess or political power. But in New York at the end of the last century it had become the predominant, or even sole, criterion. Of course, it still helped to have been born a Livingston or a Stuyvesant, and you had to show a certain decorum in matters of sex; and if you were too vulgar or boorish, people wouldn't put up with you, no matter how rich you were. But, basically speaking, any couple with a fortune that was willing to make the few concessions required could find its way into some portion of New York society. And society, furthermore, had become so grand and so ostentatious that only the very rich could afford to try to crash it. At a ball in the Proustian world of Paris one might see artists, writers, and statesmen among the members of the "old faubourg"; at Mrs. Astor's the guests seemed all to have come out of the same gilded box.

The supreme social rite of the period was not, as it would become in the 1920s and 1930s, the debutante party; it was the wedding. This was the ultimate example of Thorstein Veblen's theory of "conspicuous consumption." The wedding presents, totaling in cases as much as a million dollars, were displayed in a special chamber for the admiring guests; the newspapers speculated on the fortunes and settlements on the couple about to be joined; the church and the bride's home were converted into greenhouses of floral profusion; and, finally, the virgin bride, in diamonds and lace, escorted by her virgin bridesmaids, was given . . . to whom? To the splendid warrior who had captured her from her warrior father? For surely, in a display designed to demonstrate to the tribe which was the strongest male, the recipient of the gorgeously bedizened maiden should have been at least the equal of him who offered her. But in the mauve decade the groom, however handsome, however expensively garbed, however "conspicuous" a package himself, was apt to be the son or grandson of a tycoon and not at all a tycoon himself, and if he was the equal of his father-in-law, it was only because the latter was also the descendant of a more acquisitive forebear. The young couple seemed replicas of the little bride and groom on the wedding cake who should have been replicas of them.

How could the resumption of normal life not prove an anticlimax to both? The young men paid perfunctory visits to their offices in family businesses and gave their serious attention to sport. Their wives paid calls, organized house parties, and spent days preparing elaborate costumes for fancy dress balls. There must have been searing moments when the question "Is *this* all?" was mutely put, and their minds must have traveled back to glorious nuptials that now seemed more like a requiem.

One sees in the pages of Gertrude's diary that her husband Harry Payne Whitney's life was stained with disappointment. He never cared for business, nor did he ever find other occupations in which to use his considerable talents. There were polo and horse racing, of course, in both of which he excelled, and in his investments, ironically enough, he was gifted with a Midas touch, vastly increasing the fortune that never brought him happiness. But in the eternal round of parties that bored him there was, as for so many of his set, the solace of the bar. J Burden had a more disciplined nature; his life was strict and orderly, perhaps too much so. He clung tenaciously to a failing business without any personal economic motive, and he always organized his pleasures, like his household, with a meticulous care, but one wonders, looking at the handsome, settled features of his later photographs, if happiness did not elude him, too.

The girls, as usual in that world, did better; they were less crushed by the looming figure of an acquisitive male ancestor. Gertrude Whitney's solution, as a sculptor and museum founder, is too well known to be recorded here, and Adele's happy afterlife will be noted in the final chapter. But let us take a glance at the solutions of some of the other granddaughters—and some granddaughters-in-law—of William

Henry Vanderbilt. Adele's sister Emily, who married John
Henry Hammond, turned to God and found her release in
giving herself and her money to the cause of Moral Re-Ar-
mament, a revivalist uplift movement founded by the American Frank Buchman in the 1920s. There were those, including
her own children, who deplored her mission, but nobody who
knew her (and she lived to be ninety-four) could fail to recognize that she was happy and serene. Electra Havemeyer,
who married Adele's cousin J. Watson Webb, like Gertrude,
founded a museum. Adele's cousin Louise Shepard, who married the chemist William Jay Schieffelin, adopted the more
traditional occupation of raising nine children. And Grace
Wilson, who married Cornelius Vanderbilt III, still another
cousin, made a kind of career for herself in carrying the mauve
decade's habit of extravagant entertainment to the point of
burlesque.

The custom of seeking European coronets for the daughters
of Wall Street has long been decried as absurd and even
degrading, and it is certain that most of these alliances proved
unhappy. The American heiress was too independent—or too
spoiled—depending on which side of the ocean she was
viewed from—to adapt herself to the strict and sterile eti-
quette of feudal families. And yet there was a certain mad
logic in the ambition of a woman like Alva Vanderbilt, who
sought to re-create in a marble palace in Newport something
of the ceremonial of a European court, to marry her beautiful
daughter to an English duke. She wanted to project the Vanderbilt millions into a past that they might somehow dress up.
But she was a woman of too much energy and spirit to devote
all of her life to this idle game. In time she became a militant
suffragette who was reputed to have conceived of God as
female.

She provided, anyway, a kind of career for her daughter.
Consuelo devoted a goodly portion of her life to extricating
herself from the matrimonial cage into which her mother had
penned her. Beautiful, radiant, and possessed of a kind and
generous heart, the eighteen-year-old Duchess of Marl-

borough was loved by everyone in England but the duke. "I cannot abide tall women," he retorted to a man who had praised his wife's beauty. "Of course, I cannot say what a beast my first husband was," Consuelo remarked pensively, half a century later, to a friend with whom she was discussing her proposed memoirs.

Years after she had finally left the duke, Consuelo fell in love with Jacques Balsan, a Frenchman who had been an aviator in the First World War, and was confronted with the problem of having to obtain an annulment of her first marriage as well as a divorce, for Balsan was a strict Roman Catholic. The annulment procedure before the Sacred Roman Rota attracted wide publicity, as the petitioner had not only been united for years to her first husband, but had borne him two sons, but Alva Vanderbilt (now Belmont) atoned for her earlier maternal brutality by taking the stand and admitting to the world that she had "forced" her child to marry the duke. Consuelo was able at last to wed the man of her choice in his church and live happily ever after. But she was middle-aged before she attained her goal, and few of her titled *consoeurs* had even that luck.

17

The Diary:
January 1, 1895, to
August 12, 1896

Another year of my life! The fullest, most deeply serious and happiest year of any. This time next year where will I be? When the clouds and shadows do come to me, I must be very brave and strong for all this sunshine.

The last days of the old year were such perfect ones. We went up to Lenox early Thursday morning, J [Burden] with us, and he and I spent three more than heavenly days together. All my latent love and affection has suddenly come to the surface with a tremendous rush; it is more even than I imagined it would be. And J is lovelier than I ever thought anyone could be to me. I believe in him and trust him absolutely and love him more than I can say. I have his ring on my finger, which stands for all the promises I have made him.

Most of the family know about us, and the excitement among them is very funny to see. We are not going to announce it until the fourteenth of January, almost two weeks yet. We wrote quite a number of notes together while we were in Lenox, but they are not to be sent until the day before. I wonder if Harry [Whitney] will be very surprised. I wish I did not have all these long days every week when I could not see J. He writes me twice a day and I him, but I miss him all the time. We are going to be married early in June, and then he has promised to take me around the world. It all sounds too perfect to be true, too much like some ideal dream. But dreams sometimes are verified, and perhaps this one will be. Oh, I am so absolutely happy and glad about everything! I am excited all the time, but not nervously, restlessly excited as I used to be. On the contrary, I have a great feeling of peace in me, a feeling that I am right and true. There has not been a question or a doubt in my mind since I said yes to J, a single wondering of any kind.

How I wish we could have had more of those Lenox days together. The country could not have been more beautiful. It snowed hard all day Thursday, and we drove over from Pittsfield (J and I in the sleigh) in a blinding snowstorm. Friday there was a cloudless sky and a bright sun, though the thermometer was five below zero. We drove together in the morning in a cutter and in the afternoon walked up to the house, and sat in the bay window of my room together watching the sunset.

I am so glad his father and mother like me; they both are too lovely to me. I went up with him the other day to see them and it was so nice being in his home. The quotation of "true love never runneth smooth" is quite false; ours has run so far very smoothly and still I am sure it is very, very true.

I have been sitting before my fire this evening thinking. Then I got all Mr. [Freddy] Beach's letters, read each one through and burnt it as I finished it. It is better so, for every time I see them or read them, it makes me feel so fearfully. I do not know whether to write him or not. I have seen him only twice since he has been home, but he has not spoken to me.

Somehow or other it is hard to talk to everyone nowadays.

I wish I did not have to go to anything but the opera. Last winter I was crazy about it all, dances, dinners, everything: that was because it satisfied the restless dissatisfied spirit in me. But this winter it is different. I cannot help but think the entire time of this great new step in my life and all that it means. It is impossible to jump over to small trivial things and appear interested and contented. Consequently I am seeing very little of anyone.

Monday, January 14.

Our engagement is announced! No need for any more denying. We had our photos taken together this morning and then went to call at the Winthrops', home for luncheon, and then a two hours' drive in the light wagon with the little horses—such a perfect drive! Tonight Fred Winthrop, V. Hall, and A. Stokes dined with us. After dinner they all went off to the opera, and J, Fred Winthrop, and I had a most delightfully cozy evening together; he has just gone and J and I are alone! On this evening of the announcement of our engagement I tell you, my dearest, that I love you with all my heart, with all my soul and with all my strength, and always will so love you, amen.

Tuesday, January 29.

J has just telegraphed me from Troy that he has the grippe and will not be able to come down for the Bends' dinner this evening. I have been foolish enough to cry about it. He went to Troy Sunday night, the first time since our engagement was announced, and all yesterday and all today I have been looking forward to seeing him this evening, counting the hours and minutes, and now he is not coming, and what is worse, he is ill. I feel too fearfully to speak. If he were only in town, I could at least be near him, and probably see him, but way off in Troy—it is too maddening. I know more than ever how frightfully I have learned to love him, how passionately with every feeling in me, more than my wildest imagination ever told me I could love. He must be well enough to come

tomorrow. Oh, God, please make it so! I want him so fearfully much.

Wednesday, 7 P.M., *January 30*.

I expect J every minute. I am sure he ought not to have come
down, but oh, I am so glad. Marguerite Shepard is very ill
with pneumonia, much worse than Lila was last winter, and
there is an atmosphere of anxiety and worry in the house.[1]
Loulie Baylies was giving J and me a dinner this evening; it is
unfortunate that we should both have to give out. I had read
such a peculiar book today called *The Green Carnation*. Some
people think it is written by Oscar Wilde, or is a burlesque on
him; it is certainly most extraordinary.[2] It is impossible to
keep my mind on anything solid nowadays, and I have given
up all hope of it.

Thursday, 10 A.M., *January 31*.

Marguerite died at seven o'clock this morning. It seems all too
hard and unbearable to think of, like an agonizing nightmare.
I have been up almost all night long. We sat and watched in
her room. Is there anything which can give more intense pain
than to sit helplessly by and see a child struggle with life and
then finally give the struggle up? I have grown years older in
this one night, for I have never before felt such real sorrow,
such real suffering, and felt the real presence of death. I am
more sure than ever that without prayer one could not stand
these things. The rebellious thoughts will come up and the
questions be asked, but underneath it all our faith lasts, and
one must pray.

LATER. I have just been in with Marguerite, part of the time
alone. It is very solemn and very wonderful to be alone with
death that way, and in this case strangely beautiful. She looks
so dear, lying on the bed all in white with flowers around her
and a large daisy plant on the table by her side. My heart

---

[1] Marguerite, who was fourteen years old, was Adele's first cousin; Lila
here is Adele's youngest sister.
[2] It was, in fact, a satire on Wilde written by the English novelist Robert
Hichens, who later wrote the best-selling *The Garden of Allah*.

aches for Aunt Margaret [Shepard]; it seems as if she had
more than she could bear, and yet she can bear it. God never
gives us more than is equal to our strength.

Monday, February 11.

More than a week has passed since I last wrote. There has
been sadness in all the days, but just now my happiness is far
stronger than any sorrow. I wish I could give some of it to all
the people who want it so much, for I have never felt more
like helping others, and trying to make them glad and strong
enough to bear their sorrows. I do not think real happiness
makes one selfish; self-absorbed perhaps at times but not
selfish in one's heart. I am glad that J and I were together
those days after Marguerite died; a more serious, solemn, earnest feeling grew up between us that had not been there before. I wonder if it is possible that I should love him more than
I do now. We all start for Canada on Thursday, the family, J,
Mr. and Mrs. Baylies, Mr. Lee, Mr. Olin, and Theodore
Frelinghuysen. We expect to be gone about ten days.

Tuesday, April 9.

J and I have finally settled on the day for our wedding, the
sixth of June. How I hope the date will be kind and bless us
with a glorious day. I cannot get used to the thought that
Edith [Shepard] will not be my bridesmaid, for we have
spoken of it as being a sure thing for one of us some day, and
now it never will be. I will only have Emily, Lila, Beatrice
[Bend], Gertrude [Vanderbilt], little Ruth Twombly, and
Jessie Sloane.[3] J is going to have all Club men[4] for his ushers:
Richard Fearing, Columbus Baldwin, Nelson Perkins, Louis
Frothingham, George Blake, and Rufus Thomas; and Fred
Winthrop for best man.

Mother and I ordered the invitations yesterday. It didn't
seem a bit strange; on the contrary, I felt as if I had seen our

[3] Edith was in mourning for her sister Marguerite. Emily and Lila were
Adele's sisters; Beatrice was a friend; Gertrude, Ruth, and Jessie were
cousins.
[4] That is, fellow members of the Porcellian Club, at Harvard College.

names together for ages past. I have already had four wedding presents.

My whole visit in Troy was ideal from beginning to end. After the first day I rode every day with J two and three hours. On Friday we went way over to Burdens' lake, a third of the way to Lenox and a ride of twenty-six or -seven miles. It was a glorious day with the smell of spring in the air, and I longed more than ever to keep on staying in the country. J and I picked out various farmhouses and wondered if we could be happy living in them. I think in a certain way I could put up with such things, but in other ways I could not at all. I would hate the worry and fuss over little details, and hate the constant thought of money, economizing, fearing waste, or being cheated; it would be ghastly.

At our cooking lesson today Alice Shepard said she would like to live in a respectable tenement house for the first year of her married life and do everything herself: cook, wash, and keep house without a servant. She could stand it a week, her husband possibly three days, and then I told her there would be the saloon or the grave. All that sort of thing I have never had the slightest desire to experience myself; I much prefer the excitement of an always changing life, of travel, new scenes, new people, new experiences of all kinds—that fascinates me. It still seems too good to be true that I am actually going to have that life.

J has already engaged our stateroom on the steamer from Vancouver on the fifth of August, the *Empress of India.* I have bought a lot of books on travel and am already beginning to devour them. I had a letter from Harry Whitney the other day written in India, such a nice letter. I do hope the friendship which grew up between us so many years ago will always go on growing and never never have a setback. He said he would come over for the wedding and go back again afterward. I wonder if he really will; it would be so awfully nice of him.

I wish I were up in Troy this very minute sitting in the little smoking room with J and anticipating another long ride tomorrow. He let me ride both his English polo ponies, two of the nicest little animals I have ever sat upon. Why do good things have to end so fearfully soon? J and I have been engaged almost four months; this happens to be one good thing I want to have end, because something so much better comes afterward, and that something will never end. I wonder how it will all be just a year from today!

Scarborough. Sunday, May 12.

I spent most of last week here and came up again early yesterday morning. This will be my last Sunday with Edith until I am married. I only have three more to spend as a girl, only three weeks and four days left of my girl life. I have felt very serious and very quiet these last few days. I am realizing so much more the reality of leaving this first part of my life and starting on the second, the fuller, larger, more earnest life of the future. God help me to make it all that it now is in my dreams.

How wonderfully beautiful the country looks! The fresh green trees, the long stretches of green lawn, the orchards of white apple blossoms, the smell of lilacs, the blue violets, the wonder of it all! On Tuesday I am going up to Woodside[5] for another week and then to Lenox for the last two weeks. Tomorrow will be my last day in town, tomorrow night the last night in my room. It is very hard to be sensible and calm with all these thoughts crowding on me. Mr. [Chauncey] Depew gave me a dinner Friday night, also the last dinner I go to as a girl.

My wedding presents are beginning to come in faster and faster, over thirty now. The ones from Papa and Mamma and Uncle Corneil and Aunt Alice have completely taken away my breath. Papa gave me a gorgeous diamond sun, the largest one I have ever seen. Mother gave me a diamond and sapphire necklace, one that she has worn a little while herself and therefore all the dearer to me, and from Uncle Corneil a most gorgeous stomacher of diamonds and one enormous pearl.

---

[5] The Burdens' residence in Troy.

They sent it to me last Sunday evening, and I was so excited about it that I made J take me up in a hansom to the house so that I could thank them myself. Then we went up to J's house to show it to his father and mother. And he got me there his present for me and showed it to me first in the hansom by the glare of a street lamp. It is the loveliest diamond necklace, set in the most beautiful way. I can wear it as a collar, a tiara, or a pin. It is too dear of him to have given it to me; that and my engagement ring in one year are certainly enough to turn my head and quite spoil me.

LATER. Edith and I have just come back from a walk together and such a nice long long talk. I am sure that the talk we had that day in Marguerite's still quiet room, with her peaceful white face smiling near us, brought us closer together than we had been in years. I only hope that we will never grow apart again, never lose the sympathy which makes the perfect understanding of friendship. A woman in her married life needs her friends just as much, perhaps more than when she was a girl. The sun has just set behind the hills, and there is such a beautiful glow of light on the river. There is such a tremendous happiness inside of me that the world seems almost supernaturally beautiful.

New York. Sunday, May 12.

Three weeks [and four days] from today will be my wedding day! The invitations all went out yesterday; people are receiving them this morning. It sometimes seems all so very queer. How often on receiving wedding invitations I have wondered how my name would look, and what name would be under it. At Georgie Benjamin's wedding, standing right next to her, I almost felt as if it was myself repeating the answers I will make soon in reality. I wonder if I will be frightened. I wonder if it will seem as solemn as it does to think of it in the abstract. J and I want to come here afterward, but he is not sure if he can arrange it. The next day we go down to Biltmore to spend ten days in the dear little house George [Vanderbilt] has given to us. How perfect it will be! Then we expect to visit Lila Webb for a few days, then Lenox for two weeks, then the Adirondacks with the Twomblys for five days, then home again, and then the start for our trip around the world.

I cannot conceive of a happier girlhood than the one I have had. From beginning to end there have only been a few dark clouds which served afterward to make the sunshine all the brighter. The whole atmosphere of my home stands out in my memory without a blur in it. Papa and Mother have done everything in the world for me; I never recall having my will seriously thwarted or crossed; I never have been made unhappy. Emily all her life has been simply the personification of unselfishness, and Lila is too dear. Malcolm[6] has looked up to me as the oldest sister whom he has had to more or less obey. My childhood was all sunshine; I can recall now so many, many things about it.

Three years in the gay world have been quite enough for me to amuse myself in, to see people, to know people more or less, to learn things by experience, to make mistakes, to hurt myself, and then come out of it, perhaps some the worse for a scar. And then to have it all end the way it is ending. To be glad myself, beyond all words, to have everyone else glad; to feel that it is right and the greatest, truest step in my life. I must go down on my knees and thank God for it all, and ask Him to help me show my thankfulness in more than mere words, and ask Him to help me live out the rest of my life to its absolute fullness and uttermost capacity. These will be almost the closing words of this journal; I begin a new one the day I am married.

Elm Court, Lenox. Sunday, June 2.

Now it is *this week!* My last Sunday and my last so many other things. I feel horribly sentimental. All through the service in church today I kept saying, "The next time I am here, the next time I hear a sermon . . . !" And so it is with everything; I suppose it is natural. I feel like hanging on to all the hours, and still I want them to go, and I am crazy for Thurs-

[6] Adele's brother, the youngest of the Sloane children.

Adele, painted by Alfred Munnings, c. 1925.

day to come. Thoughts, memories, associations all rush in on me one on top of the other. Outwardly I believe I am quite calm and indifferent; I hope I can keep this up through Thursday, for as soon as you let yourself go for even a minute, it is impossible to get back the same amount of control as before.

My heart did rush up into my mouth and eyes yesterday when Emily gave me the present she has made for me, a whole year book, three hundred and sixty-five days, with quotations for every day which she has collected herself and then written out. I was simply overcome by it, am still now when I look at it here before me and realize the hours of work she has put in it. It is dedicated to both J and myself.

Unfortunately, he will not see it for two days yet. He went to town Friday afternoon to attend Belmont Tiffany's and Fannie Cameron's wedding yesterday. I have just had a letter from him telling me about it. They were engaged about the same time we were, and so we called each other the "F F F F," the First Four Finest Fiancés, rather silly, but we have kept it up all winter, though I have seen very little of them, having been in mourning most of the winter. Now that they are married, it makes me feel as if my wedding were almost here.

The weather has been beautiful but very warm for a whole week; it can't last much longer this way; I wish it would storm tomorrow or the day after and then clear off cooler, but the predictions are still warmer weather and rain toward the end of the week. Well, there is no use fussing, we can only hope for good luck. I have now two hundred and fifty-three presents; it seems to me they must have all come.

The family arrive tomorrow and the day after; then it will really seem as if the time were here.

RED LETTER DAY

Thursday, 9 A.M., *June 6.*

My wedding day!! A glorious morning, blue sky, sunshine, cold fresh air. Thank God for it! Thank God for all my past life, for all my perfect girlhood, for everything that has come to me, and help me to love my new life in its truest, highest meaning. These are the last words of my book. This is the last day in this room by myself. Last night a thousand thoughts were rushing through my mind. Tonight? Once more I love J with all my heart and soul. I am absolutely happy! The thought of really leaving home gives me a sinking feeling, of course, but I have only given away to that feeling once or twice, and I don't want to today. This greatest day of my life must be only full of brightness. Mother, Papa, Emily, Lila,

Malcolm, Edith, everyone is perfect to me, more than perfect.

[The diary here has an understandable gap of seven months.]

Lucknow, British India. Tuesday, December 31.

The last day of the old year! And instead of writing at night the closing words in my journal before beginning a new page and a new year, I am stopping home this morning, for tonight we shall be on the train approaching Agra, and shall see the first minutes of the New Year in that place. I wish the Taj could be in view, for it will be a full moonlight night, and what a sight to be greeted with the first hour of the year!

I saw the year out last December 31 and realized, or tried to realize, all that the coming year had in store for me. But no girl can imagine what her married life is really like. It is a far greater change than one thinks it, and greater still as the time goes on, and new things come to me, and the knowledge grows of what a different thing one's life is to what it used to be. Mine has always been very full of happiness, but it is more full now than ever, much more full than it was this time last year.

I think just lately that J and I have grown more closely together than ever. At first there can't help but be little scars from the friction of two separate things coming together, and however little the scars, they manage to hurt, if only for a few minutes. Then there came to us the knowledge of this third life which neither of us wanted. We had each other and could not bear the thought of anything in between. It was foolish, but I could not put down the rebellious feelings in me. I did not want a child. All our plans for this year were so perfect, and now they would be spoiled. As it is, they have not been spoiled. I am well all the time, and it is only one more thing in the long list of what I have to be thankful for. We gave up going to Java; that was the only change in our plans, and from Egypt we shall have to go straight to Paris instead of Constantinople and Greece. I expect the kid about the second week in May, and we shall spend all May and June in

Paris, probably taking an apartment there. I don't realize it at all. This next year will have changes for me and new experiences as well as the closing one has had, but not as great, and not as many. God keep and help me through them all and teach me the many new lessons I must learn, and let me think of the new life as a sacred gift and a holy trust, and may it prove a strong link in the chain that binds J and me together.

> *Hôtel des Réservoirs, Versailles.*
> *Monday, August 10, 1896.*

My little baby died at half past four o'clock this morning. Almost every minute since I have been sitting near her, kissing her, and longing with an intense longing to take her and hold her in my arms, until this aching pain inside of me went away. Can I say that I think all this is for the best? If it is for my good, why did a poor little innocent baby have to suffer three short months and then die? But no, I will not ask these questions. If I did not believe that God had taken my baby and that I was to see her again some day, I am sure that I could not sit here beside her hour after hour, feeling that I had lost her forever, without going almost crazy with grief. As it is, I know now that she is my first strong link to the future life. The baby has been with me just a year, and I still feel strongly that she is a part of my very life. It seems strange to think that now her little soul will develop its own distinct life.

She is lying in her blue cradle, with her little lace dress and blue bows at the sleeves, and her bonnet with blue ribbons. Around her head are white flowers, daisies and irises, and a tiny white rose in her hand. I never saw her look so pretty, and her little hands are like exquisitely carved pieces of ivory.

J and I are quite alone. I am glad. It is so much easier with him than with anyone else, and then I have the baby all to myself. I scarcely realize that she has really gone, for the last fortnight she has seemed like a little angel on earth, and it was a very small step to bring a little angel in heaven. I cried my heart out for two hours and now I feel quiet. I don't pray very much, and yet I feel that strength is being given to me. I know how Mother must feel for me, and I long to see her.

Tuesday, August 11.

It seems so strange to be receiving all the home cables of sympathy from just the same people who three months ago were sending us congratulatory messages.

I am still sitting with the little baby and hate to be away from her a minute. I can't realize how soon it will all be over. I don't feel yet as if she had quite gone from me yet. God help me through tomorrow. She is lying in a mass of tiny white rosebuds; hanging above her head is a wreath of white vines, marguerites, with roses at the top, and there are vases of white daisies and carnations and roses around her.

16 avenue de l'Alma, Paris. Wednesday, August 12.

It is all over, and I am almost too tired to think. I sat up with the baby from twelve to one o'clock last night and then was up again this morning at seven. Shall I ever forget my last hour with my baby? I put her into her little casket myself, and J and I arranged the flowers around her. In her right hand I put a white rose and he a white carnation. Then we kissed her over and over and prayed God to help us, and I kissed her again. A little before nine they took her away, and at half past nine J and I drove in [to Paris]. The last time I had taken that drive was when I brought the baby out to Versailles a month ago, and how dear she was all the way! We came here to the apartment, which had been left open for us, and then went right to the church. Mrs. Burden met us at the door. She had just arrived from Hamburg. George was in the chapel and Mr. and Mrs. [Robert] Bacon. There was no one else but the servants. The baby's casket was covered with flowers and there were flowers all around. A large wreath from Papa and Mamma, a white cross from Mr. and Mrs. Burden, wreaths from George [Vanderbilt] and Loulie Baylies, and flowers from Emily, Lila, and Malcolm and the Bacons. Our wreath was at her head. At eleven-thirty Dr. Thurber began the service. He read beautiful passages from the Bible, made a short address and a prayer. I chose the hymns that I had sung most often to the baby: "Jesus Calls Us o'er the Tumult" and "There's a Wideness in God's Mercy." I used to sing them to her almost every day. After the service was over we waited to put her in the Mortuary Chapel which is next the chancel. It was all filled with green palms, and we left the baby there in the midst of all her flowers. It is better not to speak about my loneliness without her.

18

"Living Well Is the Best Revenge"

Fortunately Adele did not have to lose another child. Her next two children were sons, James A. Burden III, and W. Douglas Burden, the explorer and naturalist, who both lived into their eighties, and her fourth child, Shiela, now Mrs. Blake L. Lawrence, survives. Adele and her husband decided to settle in New York as J Burden's duties in Troy were not so extensive as to require the presence of his family there, and it was obvious that they would need a house, and a large one. At the turn of the century the well-to-do in Manhattan did not rent or buy; they built.

Andrew Carnegie had purchased land on both sides of Ninety-first Street and Fifth Avenue, and on the south side he had erected the heavy, brick mansion that houses the Cooper-Hewitt Museum today, one of the few private residences in Manhattan to have its own large garden. Carnegie was happy to sell two of the northern lots to William Douglas Sloane, son of his old friend William, who at the turn of the century proceeded to build two large beaux arts houses for his daughters Adele and Emily. These stand today, and Ninety-first Street remains a witness to how much better the poor Scots

No. 642 Fifth Avenue, the New York residence of Adele's parents. Her bedroom was on the third story to the far left.

weavers did when they crossed the Atlantic to the new world. Adele arranged her house for extensive entertainment; it had a ballroom in the style of the Galerie des Glaces at Versailles on the third story. Into this habitation she moved, at the age of twenty-seven, with twenty-seven servants and gave parties she enjoyed as much as her guests did.

Adele was something of a musician, and she preferred musical evenings to dinner parties, which must have been an improvement over the usual, heavy eight-course dinners of the day. Also, she looked for interesting and amusing people—she entertained the composer Giacomo Puccini and Mark Twain. Next door, Emily, who went in for good works and served no alcohol, gave less lively soirées; the friends that the sisters had in common would drop in at Adele's for a cocktail and a laugh to assist them through the more rigorous evening at Emily's.

Adele, like her mother, who with her husband established the Sloane Maternity Hospital, now part of the Columbia-Presbyterian Medical Center, engaged in many charitable activities, but that is not the aspect of her life that I seek to emphasize here. What concerns me is what was nearest to her heart: how she dealt with the situation of having been given both time and money and no real guidelines as to how to use either. Her solution might have been inspired by the mordant Spanish proverb that was such a favorite of Gerald Murphy, the epicurean friend of the Scott Fitzgeralds: "Living well is the best revenge."

Adele accomplished this in the finest sense. Whatever she did, she did well, and, enjoying it, she gave pleasure to others. In 1917 she built a handsome Georgian house, Woodside Acres, in Syosset, Long Island, and created gardens that became famous in horticultural circles. She loved riding and hunted on Long Island, as well as in Ireland and England; she became a leading figure in the Meadowbrook Hunt. When she traveled to Europe, she was always up at dawn for a first glimpse of the coastline, no matter how many times she had seen it before or how late she had been up playing bridge. She spoke French, Italian, and some German. She was one of the founders and an early president of the Colony Club.

I recall the night when, then in her eighty-fourth year, she told me that she was through with dining out. She came home from a party, looking magnificent in a parure of aquamarines, sat quietly on the sofa for a few minutes, and then said: "I'm not going out any more. The time has come." There was no bitterness in her tone, hardly a note of regret. It was simply an acceptance of failing power, with the resolution never to seem laborious.

Adele with Shiela Burden, 1903.

Adele's children, 1902: Shiela, James, and Douglas Burden.

Four generations, 1958: Adele (right), with her daughter Shiela Burden Lawrence (left), her granddaughter Adele Lawrence Auchincloss, and great-grandson John W. Auchincloss II.

Emily Vanderbilt Sloane White, Adele's mother, on her ninetieth birthday, in 1932, surrounded by all her children and grandchildren and by some of the spouses of the latter. Mrs. White is in the center, holding a bouquet, between her daughters Lila Sloane Field (on her right) and Emily Sloane Hammond. Adele, the oldest daughter, is seated on Lila's right.

Adele in California, 1936.

Adele with James A. Burden III, 1898.

J with James A. Burden III, 1898.

Adele as president of the Colony Club, 1935.

J in his fifties.

Adele in middle age.

J and Adele with their daughter, Shiela, in the late 1920s.

Woodside Acres, Syosset, Long Island, Adele's home after 1917.

The gardens at Woodside Acres.

Adele with her cousin Electra Webb Bostwick, in Paris, 1953.

Adele's granddaughter Adele Lawrence, at her wedding to Louis Auchincloss, September 7, 1957.

Adele at her granddaughter Adele's wedding, with her niece Mrs. Benny Goodman, September 7, 1957.

Adele with her second husband, Richard M. Tobin, late 1930s.

Last photograph of Adele with her great-grandson John W. Auchincloss II, 1959.

I believe that Adele never quite understood why her first husband had to devote so much of his time to a declining family business in Troy. The Burden ironworks, which had specialized in horseshoes, never recovered from the advent of the automobile. When she went abroad to her house in Paris, leaving him to what she must have considered dreary days in Troy, it was her greatest regret that he would not give it all up and go with her. After all, she had more than enough for both! Perhaps her second husband, Dick Tobin, himself a musician, an amateur of the arts, a favorite in international society, was basically the more congenial of her two spouses, but in her last years, again a widow, her thoughts kept returning to the earlier days, and when she died she left directions that she be buried with J in the Burden mausoleum in Troy.

Appendix

The *Journal*, Lincoln, Nebraska, May 26, 1895

A BILLION DOLLAR WEDDING
The Marriage of W. H. Vanderbilt's Granddaughter
UNHEARD OF SPLENDORS

The Recent Gould Affair Thrown Utterly into the Shade by This Coming Event of Fashion and Money

The Legislature of a great State [Illinois] played to posterity not so many days ago by an official entreaty to nubile heiresses to bestow themselves, or, rather, their inheritances, upon Americans only. There is a wedding coming off on the 6th of June which will certainly be the marriage of the year—not even excepting the recent Gould nuptials—and it will be a strictly American affair, notwithstanding the fact that the bride's mother is worth $20,000,000 and that the groom is a young Croesus. The bride-to-be has two uncles worth $80,000,000 apiece, and half a dozen worth $20,000,000 each. But as she is to wed a plain American citizen, nobody has given much attention to the affair. Had Miss Adele Sloane given herself to a penniless grandee from the other side, she would no doubt be famous by this time.

An engagement of Miss Sloane to James A. Burden, Jr., was announced last February. The wedding is to take place at Lenox, Massachusetts.

But before entering into that part of the matter, it is well to observe that this is to be strictly a Vanderbilt occasion. Miss Sloane, as has been remarked time and again, is the second of the grandchildren of the late W. H. Vanderbilt to wed. The young lady is the daughter of William D. Sloane, who married a daughter of the late millionaire and got $15,000,000 by the performance. Mr.

Sloane himself is worth many millions in his own right, however. This is his daughter's third season "out." She has been the centre of a whirl of gayeties for weeks at the Court, the superb Sloane country seat at Lenox. Then she is entertained, too, at Wyndhurst, the house of Mr. John Sloane, her multi-millionaire uncle. In addition to that, another uncle of Miss Sloane's, Cornelius Vanderbilt, has leased the Bacon cottage at Lenox. Then Mr. and Mrs. James Abercrombie Burden, parents of the groom and millionaires both, have taken the fine Eddy cottage for the season, and their affairs in honor of the approaching event are beyond description. Miss Sloane herself drives out daily in her famous four-in-hand drag. The fair girl is an expert with the whip, in addition to being an expert in archery and a devotee of all outdoor sports.

The wedding, taking into account the presents and the dresses and the functions, will represent an outlay of over $1,000,000. The Goulds beggared description at the de Castellane affair, but the Vanderbilts will certainly send it to the almshouse. A mere list of the people who will attend—and there will be guests by the train load—would read like the cream of the income tax lists. Mr. William Douglas Sloane has already made arrangements to have two hundred wedding guests accommodated at Curtis Hotel alone. A vestibuled train will bring up the New York guests, the day before the wedding family: George Vanderbilt, the bride's bachelor uncle; Mr. and Mrs. F. W. Vanderbilt, who, alas, have no children; Dr. Seward Webb; the whole Shepard contingent; and the H. McK. Twomblys will complete the Vanderbilt delegation. That is, of course, excepting the Willie K. Vanderbilts. Nobody knows exactly how the Willie K.'s will be disposed of. They have certainly asked *him*, and he was supposed to go with his daughter Consuelo, but that young lady will not go without her mamma, and her mamma was not asked. That, at least, is the way the gossips put it. Little Harold S. Vanderbilt is to be a page, and Willie K., Jr., is to be there at any rate. But if Mrs. Alva Vanderbilt were there and happened to meet Mr. Willie it would be embarrassing. One is curious to know how it will be settled, but one hates to ask.

The bride's wedding dress was made by Worth, or, rather, by his sons. It is of heavy satin, ivory colored, trimmed with point lace, thirteen inches wide, Bretonne pattern. The train is round and eleven feet long. The gown is lined throughout with heavy satin, fashioned at the bottom with lace ruffles, trimmed with bows of satin ribbon. A large drapery flows over the bodice. The sleeves are exceptionally wide, very full at the top, and taken in at the underpart, buttoning closely over the waist. The bodice of the gown fastens at the back, under a roll of satin and two bows of lace. The bridal veil is of very rare old lace, fastened at the crown of the head with a bunch of orange blossoms.

Turning to less important things, it may be mentioned that this young woman and this young man are very much in love. The match was first suggested over a year ago, but the fond pair have been compelled to wait until time could prove the fidelity and strength of an eternal attachment, as they say in old-fashioned story books. Time having proved the same, all is well. The bride's dowry will be a cool million—why is a million always cool?—and the bridegroom inherits another cool million from his grandmother, besides which are numerous billionaire uncles and aunts, and a veritable frigid expanse of cool millions in all directions.

All in all, it will be the wedding of the year. We Americans may feel proud of the fact that the wedding of the year is to be so strictly American an affair. To their credit, be it said, the weddings of the Vanderbilts always are. W. H. Vanderbilt's children wedded Americans. His grandchildren, so far, have done the same. The millionaire dynasty is a strictly native one, and the family policy is said to be that it ever shall. May the Legislature of Illinois remember this circumstance, and be comforted.

[*Editor's Note:* November 6 of that same year witnessed the marriage of Consuelo Vanderbilt to the Duke of Marlborough.]